# The Art and Science of
# FLY FISHING

# The Art and Science

## of

# FLY FISHING

## H. LENOX H. DICK, M.D.

### with drawings by

ALAN PRATT

D. VAN NOSTRAND COMPANY, INC.

Princeton, New Jersey

D. VAN NOSTRAND COMPANY, INC.
120 Alexander St., Princeton, New Jersey (*Principal office*)
24 West 40 Street, New York, New York    10018

D. VAN NOSTRAND COMPANY, LTD.
358 Kensington High Street, London, W.14, England

D. VAN NOSTRAND COMPANY (Canada) LTD.
25 Hollinger Road, Toronto 6, Canada

To my father-in-law

SPENCER BIDDLE

# Acknowledgments

KNOWLEDGE is based on the discoveries of our predecessors. In writing this book I utilized the teachings of Spencer Biddle, coupled with a review of the fishing literature, going back to the works of Halford in the '90s and continuing up through Skues, Hewitt, La Branch, Tavner . . . until the present time.

As I look back over my 20-year association with Mr. Biddle I have often wondered what did he precisely teach me and I have trouble. Then I realize why. This man was so modest and he taught me in such a manner that I felt I had discovered these things for myself. The one concrete fact I know I learned was the unity of fly fishing, dry fly, wet fly and nymph fishing are one and the same.

I wish to express my appreciation to my wife for her patience and assistance during the course of writing this book.

The illustrator, Alan Pratt, is a master fly fisherman with the unique ability to read water and express it in his illustrations. Fortune smiled on this book when he consented to do the illustrations.

I would especially like to single-out Pete Hidy, author of Sports Illustrated's book on wet fly fishing. It was his initial encouragement that gave me the impetus to start to write. During the course of my writing Pete presented me with many valuable suggestions.

Fred Lock, of the Oregon State Game Commission and Stanley Jewett of the U.S Fish and Wildlife Service rewrote the Chapter on Entomology.

Wayne Busek, Dan Bailey and Dr. Nat Wilson gave me valuable assistance with nymph patterns.

Finally, I wish to express my appreciation to all the members of the Oregon Fly Fishers Club who, over the years, have given so freely of their lore and experiences.

# Contents

# List of Illustrations

## Introduction

THE ART OF FLY FISHING is the skill and grace with which the angler casts his fly. The science of fly fishing uses the knowledge of where fish are, how they feed and proper fly presentation. If the science of fly fishing is neglected trout are not caught regularly. This science may seem complex but can be reduced to the ability to read water and proper fly presentation.

There is no single way of fishing each of the various types of fly. A streamer can be fished as a dry fly; a nymph as a streamer. Nature presents food to trout in all these manners. We must constantly imagine how she would do it at a given time, place and season.

The halftone and color plates that accompany this text place the reader at streamside. The text and line illustrations teach him to read water, locate the trout and then properly present his fly. Other important facts of fly fishing are also discussed.

A trout hooked on a small fly and played on a light, whippy fly rod brings out and magnifies every action. The thrill of landing a trout with a fly has a certain zest that cannot be duplicated by the same action with bait.

A fish caught on a fly may be returned to the stream and live while one caught on bait usually dies. Civilization has gravely reduced the fish population, especially species like trout which require cold, clear water. If we are to preserve stream trout fishing for future generations we must fish for fun and not for food.

PART ONE

*Fundamentals*

# CHAPTER 1

## *Basic Tackle*

Only balanced equipment will cast a fly properly. I urge you to heed the following advice:

*Basic Fly Rod*—The illustrated graph, Fig. 1, represents a composite of favorite rods, mine and Spencer Biddle's, for average trout fishing. When the time comes to select the rod, either purchase one of those listed or hang a two-ounce weight on the tip of your prospective choice and construct a graph of its action similar to Fig. 1.

*MacKenzie #86*—Weight: 3¾ oz.; Length: 8½ ft.; 2-piece fiberglass rod; Line: HCH-DT6-F or S. MacKenzie Rod Co., 4717 N.W. Barnes Road, Portland, Oregon.

*Fenwick Ferlite #84*—Weight: 4⅛ oz.; Length: 8½ ft.; 2-piece fiberglass rod; Line: HCH-DT6-F or S. Fenwick Products, Inc., 1207 Euclid Ave., Long Beach. California.

*Garcia #2637T*—Weight: 4½ oz.; Length: 8 ft.; 2-piece fiberglass rod; Line: GBG-DT7-F or S. Garcia Corp., 329 Alfred Ave., Teaneck, N.J., 07666.

The MacKenzie rod I have used for twelve years and the Fenwick for two years. The Fenwick is the finest rod I have ever used, including bamboo. Prices range from $15.00 to about $30.00.

*Fly Lines*—Since World War II fly lines have been vastly improved. It is difficult to purchase a bad fly line in the better grades. I have been using Scientific Lines and Courtland Lines whose addresses are:

3

*Scientific Anglers, Inc.,* Midlands, Michigan
*Courtland Line Co.,* 67E Court St., Courtland, N. Y., 13046

Recently I have experimented with inexpensive Herter Fly
Lines. *Herter's Masterweave Floating Fly Line* will cast ade-

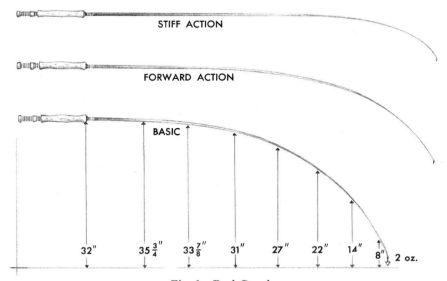

STIFF ACTION

FORWARD ACTION

BASIC

32″    35 3/4″    33 7/8″    31″    27″    22″    14″    8″    2 oz.

Fig. 1   Rod Graph

quately. Herter also sells a masterweave sinking line at the
same price. I have not tried this. I suspect that their *Supreme
Fly Lines,* HCH, sinking and floating, may be as good as many
of the better grade lines although I have not tried them.
Address:

*Herter's, Inc.,* Waseca, Minnesota

The fishing techniques in this book are predicated on the
premise that the fly fisherman will have both a floating and a
sinking line available at all times. I prefer a double tapered
line for 90% of all trout fishing. A rule of thumb: Choose a

line one size heavier than that recommended by the manufacturer. When you become expert you can go back to the lighter line. I never have.

*Fly Reels*—Fly reels serve only to hold line and do not participate in actual fly casting. There is only one reason for owning a moderately-priced reel instead of an inexpensive one. Big fish! Any fish much over 10 inches should be played from the reel. Truly big trout, three pounds or over, may make long runs. The bearings of a cheap reel may bind and away goes the fish!

I have used Pflueger Medalist reels for 25 years and they are my standard for comparison. Recently, an inexpensive reel has come on the market made of polypropylene plastic. I have examined this reel but have not used it. It should stand up.

*Pflueger Medalist #1495*—Enterprise Mfg. Co., Akron, Ohio
*Weber Craft #500*—Weber Tackle Co., Stevens Point, Wisconsin (Polypropylene Plastic)

Remember to purchase an extra spool with your reel.

*Leaders*—A leader is a long strand of nylon or gut connecting the fly to the line. In the past fifteen years nylon has replaced the old silkworm gut leader. Nylon leaders are stronger, cast better and there is no need for soaking. The only choice today is between a limp nylon and the German platyl nylon.

Platyl is a stronger limp nylon material. It has less stretch in it than the regular limp nylon. I prefer platyl leaders because they are stronger. At the present time these are supplied only as tapered, single-strand leaders. However, if the fisherman prefers a tied leader, he may obtain this material in spools and tie his own.

The best limp nylon leaders are tied leaders similar to the old gut ones. These, when properly tied, cast a bit better than the single-strand, tapered leaders. I carry two sizes of leader;

none shorter than nine feet. These are 2X and 4X. The 'X' designation refers to the diameter of the tip, 4X being quite fine. During the course of a day's fishing one frequently changes flies, gradually shortening the tip of the leader by 6 or 8 inches. This renders the tip too heavy and thick to properly present the fly without a great deal of disturbance in the water. It then becomes necessary either to tie on a new leader or lengthen the old. I carry with me spools of 2X, 4X and 5X leader material replace the tips of the leaders. At times, I may make a 4X leader into a 10 or 11 foot 5X leader by tying on extra 5X material. This long, finely-tapered leader is used with size #18 or #20 midge flies.

Before using a leader stretch the kinks out, otherwise it will not lie straight on the water.

Enough about tackle. Fishing books, as a rule, spend too much time discussing equipment and not enough discussing fishing techniques.

# CHAPTER 2

## *Basic Fly Casting*

In fly casting, the line is cast; in lure or bait casting, the lure is cast. It is possible to take a fly line and cast it with a non-bending broom handle purely by wrist action combined with the weight and balance of the line. The actual performance resembles hammering a nail into a vertical wall, with a pause at the top of the backward stroke, allowing the line to straighten out behind. This is followed by the forward stroke. The old method of teaching concentrated on wrist action with the elbow held against the side. Today the student is instructed to keep the wrist stiff and let the elbow and shoulder do the work. However, if using your wrist comes instinctively to you, then use it. The secret of fly casting lies in the tip of

Fig. 2

the rod, Fig. 2. In the hands of an expert, fly casting appears as a smooth, graceful performance, Fig. 3, but if we break it down into its component parts, it becomes a jerky performance. If the novice will concentrate on the jerky aspects he will be able to cast an acceptable line in 15 minutes. The deliberate jerk makes the tip work and *that* is the secret. *Make the tip work* . . . Fig. 4!! First, strip 15 feet of line from the

7

Fig. 3   Expert Casting

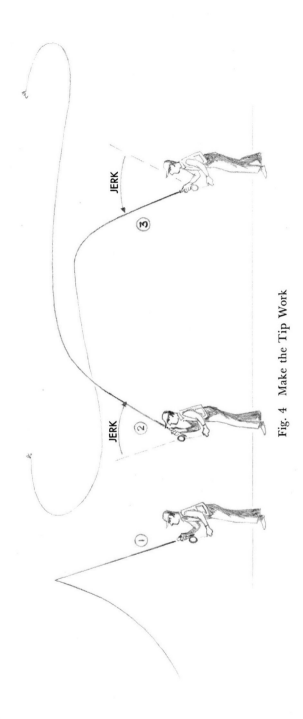

Fig. 4   Make the Tip Work

reel; it is a good idea to measure this. Hold the arm and hand in the position shown in the drawing with the rod at 10:00 o'clock position. Don't worry about the wrist, elbow and shoulder; they will instinctively take care of themselves. Instead, *concentrate on the jerky action of the tip.* Bring the rod quickly back to the 1 o'clock position, allowing the line to fall to the ground in back of you. Look around; you will find the line is straight out in back. With the rod still in the 1 o'clock position, bring it forward smartly just like hammering the nail, and stop it again at 10:00 o'clock. If you forget that it is a fly rod and pretend that you are hammering nails, *with a pause between the backward and forward stroke,* you will have the basic fundamentals of fly casting. Concentrate on making that tip work! Practice this simple maneuver for 5 minutes. Next, do not allow the line to fall on the ground but consciously turn your head as the line goes back and, before it strikes the ground, start the forward stroke. If the line cracks like a whip you are not waiting long enough to start the forward stroke.

## LENGTHENING THE LINE

Now that you have learned the fundamentals of casting, you must learn to bring in the line properly. This is accomplished by holding the line in the same hand as the rod and pulling the line in with the opposite hand. The excess line is caught and coiled in the pulling hand, Fig. 5.

To lengthen the cast, strip off line with the left hand and allow it to go back with a back cast or forward with a forward cast. This is referred to as false casting.

When I first fished with Spencer Biddle he used to turn to me with a glint in his eye and say, "Brother, three false casts are all you are allowed. After that the line falls in the water

and *you fish*, no matter how bad a cast it may be! There are no fish in the trees on this stream."

There is a point where the length of the line balances the action of the rod, after which, the line starts to fall into the water behind you. When this point is reached, borrow some of your wife's red nail polish and daub some on the line just where it comes through the top guide. This will make it easy for you to find the balance point the next time you cast. When this point is reached, if the angler desires to lengthen his cast, more line should be pulled from the reel and coiled in the

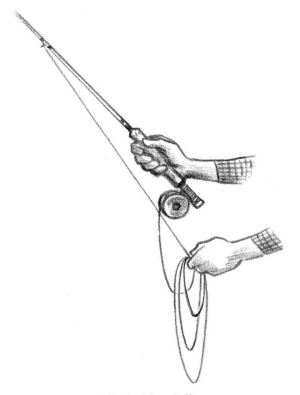

Fig. 5   Line Coils

left hand. Then, when the forward cast is reached, the line is allowed to shoot out . . . thereby lengthening the cast by many feet.

The expert angler, about to start his cast, strips from the reel the necessary amount of line that he thinks he will need for his entire cast, coils this in his left hand in loose coils, Fig. 5, makes two false casts and shoots the remainder of the line.

## THE ROLL CAST

The next basic cast the angler must learn is the roll cast, Fig. 6. This allows the fisherman to cast his line while standing next to a high bank or under a tree. If your rod is too stiff you will not cast well. The basic rod will roll cast with ease. However, the line must be balanced to the rod and it must be heavy enough. If your rod does not cast well, try a whippier or softer rod or else try a heavier line on your present rod, before you become disgusted.

Now, cast 15 feet of line in front of you and then carefully follow the illustration. Bring the rod back two feet with a straight arm so that your hand and shoulder are back and opposite each other, bring the arm and shoulder forward quickly and, at the same time, hammer that nail with your wrist. Lo! The line gracefully rolls out and you have made your first roll cast! With the proper rod and line the roll cast is a cinch!

When fishing, pick your line off the water with a roll cast before starting the next cast. This allows you to bring the fly in close, pick up 15 or 20 feet of line easily and decrease the amount of false casting necessary to shoot out the next cast.

## STRAIGHT CAST WITH 'S' CURVES

A great deal of the time the fisherman fishes upstream and allows his fly to drift down toward him in a natural manner.

In order to avoid drag it is necessary to cast upstream or down with many S curves in the line. An example of this is shown in Fig. 10 and 11.

Cast exactly as you did while performing the basic straight cast. Instead of the usual follow-through to the 10:00 o'clock position, stop the rod abruptly at 11:00 o'clock. You will note

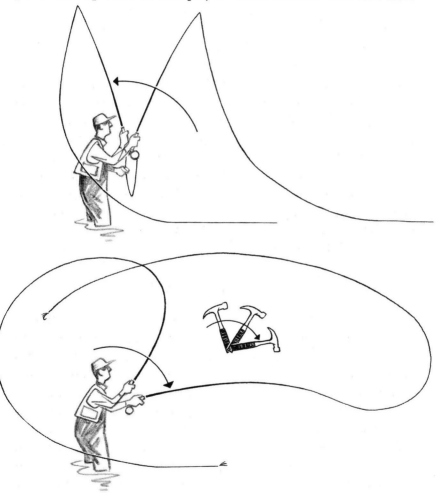

Fig. 6   Roll Cast

that the line will fall with many S curves in it. The size of the S curves can be varied by the amount of follow-through utilized.

## CURVED UPSTREAM CAST

You will frequently read in fishing literature about the curved upstream cast. This is a cast for the truly expert.

Face upstream on the left bank of the stream. Instead of holding your rod in a vertical position, hold it out from you at a 45 degree angle. Cast the fly exactly as you did with the regular fly cast we described previously. You have now performed a straight-side-arm cast. Now, cast again, but do not put sufficient power in the forward cast to straighten out the line! Voila!! You have performed a curved upstream cast.

Most fishermen are capable of performing this cast only about one-half of the time. A straight quartering upstream cast with S curves in the line will do almost as well. Whenever this cast is mentioned, keep this fact in mind. Both of these casts are used to prevent drag.

## MENDING A CAST

That old devil "drag" will plague you all your fishing career. Many times a day you will make a cast, the current will take the belly out of your line and your fly will drag. This calls for putting another curve in your line without actually recasting the line. In order to do this, we "mend" the line.

Lower the tip of your rod close to the water. At the same time take a little slack line from the reel and hold it in your left hand. Then with your rod tip make a partial side-roll-cast . . . up, over and down . . . in upstream direction, allowing at the same time, the slack line to shoot out of your left hand. This must be done with just enough power to also pick up

the part of your line that is curved downstream but not
enough to disturb the fly, Fig. 7. Another way to describe this

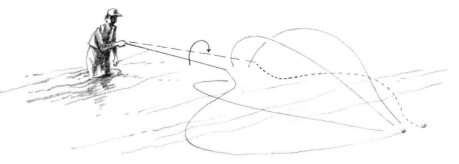

Fig. 7   Line Mending

cast is a side-arm-roll cast. This is a most valuable cast and
can be used anytime there is drag.

There are many other casts used in fly fishing . . . so many,
in fact, that when I read books on fly casting I become hopelessly confused. They are all variations of the casts I have described. When you have become proficient in their use you
will instinctively learn many others.

You will probably want to learn the Double-Haul cast in
the future. This technique will add a third more distance to
your cast. However, Spencer Biddle, the greatest practical fly
fisherman I ever watched, never consciously used the Double-
Haul.

As there are fishermen who spend most of their time tying
flies, there are fishermen who emphasize fly casting to the
detriment of the rest of their fishing prowess.

# CHAPTER 3

## *Fly Presentation*

In this book we fish together. You will be at my elbow or close-by throughout. I want you to have the feeling and mood of actual participation. Put on your waders, gather up your gear and we will go to a stream.

I would like to suggest that you always wear a fishing vest with a built-in life preserver. Once you have seen a careless fisherman floating face-down in a river you will learn to be extremely cautious about big rivers. Many of the rivers we will fish together in this book will fall into that category. The pool you and I will fish today is in a relatively small river, but it can be boated even at this stage, and fishermen have drowned during high water.

Look over Plate 4 carefully so that you have a good mental picture. Now, look at the line drawing, Fig. 20, and find the various common land marks. Remember, the pictures in this book are taken so that you are looking upstream and the water is flowing toward you.

Now, rig up your rod with your sinking or wet fly line. Tie on a nine-and-one-half-foot 2X leader and a number 10 Bucktail Coachman. Please note Fig. 8 for instruction in tying various KNOTS. The leader is heavier than you will usually use, but it will be easier to cast for your initial lesson in fly presentation.

Walk up to the pool and stand at fishing position 2; Plate 4, Fig. 20. Cast 30 feet of line straight out in front of you; watch carefully what happens to your fly and line as it swings down-

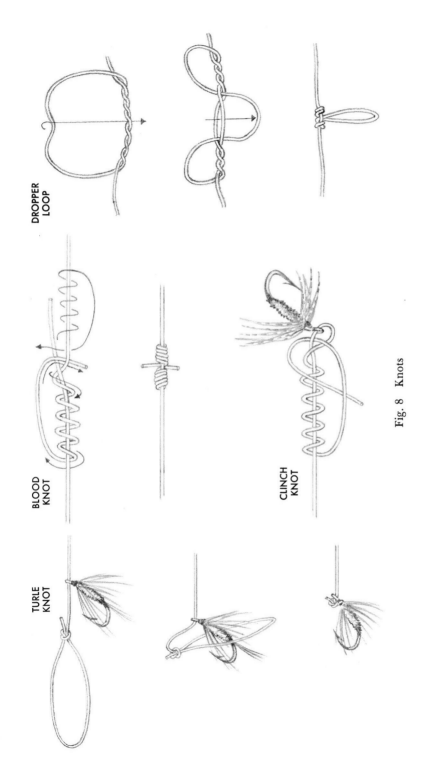

TURLE KNOT

BLOOD KNOT

DROPPER LOOP

CLINCH KNOT

Fig. 8  Knots

stream below you. A downstream belly will form in the line
and the fly will be quickly dragged around and down stream.
The fly will cover very little water. A cast straight out from
the fisherman is little used in stream fly fishing. Repeat this
cast and watch what happens to the fly and leader. The chances
are that your fly floated on the surface until it had swung well
below you. By that time the line had sunk and the fly had been
pulled under the surface. If you had actually been fishing, your
fly would have first been a floating but dragging dry fly and
then, as the line swung around and the fly sank, it would have
been a sunk wet fly with a tight line and drag. Dry and wet
flies are tied differently but they can be used interchangeably.
If this seems confusing, don't worry . . . as we fish together in
the chapters to come, this will gradually clear up.

You have seen what happens to the fly and line when cast
straight out; now, to learn to properly present your fly! This
chapter and the one on reading water are the two most important in the book. Master these and you will have mastered the
fundamentals of fly fishing. Present your fly properly, in the
right place and any of a dozen flies will catch fish for you. A
majority of fly fishermen do not know the rudiments of fly
presentation. To consistently catch fish you should know the
basic techniques of presentation. Broken down into fundamentals, these are simple techniques with numerous variations.

## QUARTERING DOWN AND ACROSS

### "Wet Fly"

Go back to where you were standing before, but instead of
casting directly across the current, turn slightly and cast the
line at a 45° angle downstream, Fig. 9. Instead of immediately
casting 30 feet of line, cast only 15 feet and allow the line to
swing down below you. Notice the difference. A belly did not

form in your line as soon as it did with the straight cast, and your fly stayed out farther in the current for a longer time.

Now the fly is below you. Bring it back with little twitches or jerks. You have now performed a quartering downstream cast—the commonest cast used in presenting a wet fly. It can also be used for streamer flies, nymph flies, nymphs and dry flies. Next time, cast about 20 feet and repeat the process. The next . . . cast 30 feet, etc. Why not cast 30 to 50 feet at the start? One of the grave errors in fly presentation is over-fishing the water or casting too long a line and thereby casting a line over a fish and putting him down before you have a chance to catch him.

Practice that cast for about 5 minutes. Remember, start fishing close to you and then gradually work your fly out. Who knows, there may be fish in that water and you might catch one.

You have practiced long enough. You are committing a grave error by picking your line up off the water too soon, because you were not satisfied with the cast. This causes a slurping effect and, again, will scare away the fish. Whenever your fly and line strike the water . . . leave them . . . and DON'T pick them up, no matter how bad the cast, until they swing downstream from you. It is surprising how many fish I've caught with casts I did not like but fished out anyway.

You are now ready for a variation in the quartering downstream presentation. Cast your fly exactly as before, but when your fly lands at 'A' allow it to drift to 'B.' At this point strip more line from the reel, thereby causing the line to slow down and stay in the middle of the current for a while longer. When the fly is below you, allow it to stop for at least a minute. Fish often strike at this point. They follow the fly until it finishes its swing and then will take it as it stops. At times they pause before taking it. If you are overly anxious you will miss the strike. Now bring the fly back with little twitches.

A final variation of the quartering downstream technique is

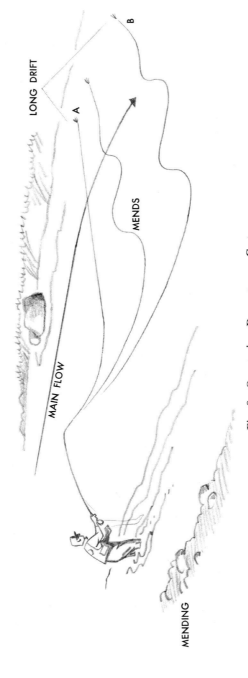

Fig. 9  Quartering Downstream Cast

as follows: Cast your fly downstream at a 45° angle. Allow it to drift a foot or two and then put a mend in your line, Fig. 9. Notice that the fly drifts downstream without drag. Each time it appears that the fly may drag, throw another mend in your line. This technique is used whenever drag is not wanted, such as presenting a dry fly or a wet fly with a natural drift.

## QUARTERING UPSTREAM

### *"Dry Fly"*

Change your line from the sinking to the floating one. Cast your fly, quartering upstream, with a few S curves in the line as shown in Fig. 10. This is the usual manner of fishing a dry fly. It is easier to make a fly float without drag when fishing upstream. An added advantage is the sounds of your wading are carried away from the fish. As the fly floats downstream retrieve some line (depending on the speed of the water); too much slack line will cause you to miss the fish if it rises for the fly. When the fly ceases its natural float, it should be allowed to swing well below before quietly retrieving the line and recasting. This is to prevent disturbing any fish that may be near you.

The technique of upstream quartering cast with a slack line may be used to fish a sunken wet fly or nymph. When cast upstream the fly sinks deeper than it would with the quarter-

Fig. 10   Quartering Upsteam Cast with Curve

ing downstream method because it does not have the pull of
the line to drag it up to the surface.

Some experts are able to cast a big upstream curve in their
lines instead of the 'S' curves we use. In the future when this
method is referred to, remember the 'S' curves are simpler and
will do as well.

## DIRECTLY UPSTREAM

### *"Dry Fly"*

The fly is cast directly upstream. It will drift straight toward you, either on the surface or at varying depths beneath
the surface. The line must be retrieved rapidly without disturbing the fly, so that you can successfully strike the fish.
This technique is particularly effective when fishing close to
the bank of a stream, Fig. 11. Occasionally it may be used in
wet fly fiishing.

Fig. 11   Upstream Cast with Curves

## DIRECTLY DOWNSTREAM

### *"Dry or Wet Fly"*

This cast is used primarily for the dry fly, Fig. 12. However, it is also used to present a nymph or wet fly with a natural float. The fisherman casts the fly in such a manner that large 'S' curves are placed in the line. The straightening-out of these 'S' curves allows the fly to float naturally until the line is straight. A further float may be obtained by stripping line from the reel and waggling the rod tip to produce more 'S' curves. This technique is particularly applicable to fishing downstream under trees and other obstructions.

Fig. 12   Downstream Cast with s curves

Variations in these four techniques will be brought out and amplified in the chapter on stream tactics. When talking to fishing experts keep in mind that there are only four basic techniques . . . then you will be able to break down their complicated discussions into one of these. Your own variations of these techniques will come instinctively as you progress in fishing.

# CHAPTER 4

## *Reading Water*

You have spent enough time practicing casting. For the next two days we will drive around to the various rivers and I will try to teach you how to read water. Obviously, the pictures used to illustrate this book were taken in different regions. They represent portions of streams in Oregon, Washington and British Columbia. However unfamiliar the terrain may appear, the basic water characteristics may be found in any stream in North America.

Fish are where you find them, sometimes where you least expect them. An inexperienced angler may read water well on one stream and be completely lost on another only a few miles away. An example: steelhead on the Rogue River, that are inclined to strike a fly, are more often found at the tail-end of pools in the region of the break, whereas, in Northern Oregon and Washington streams, they seem to lie more toward the head of the pool. In a few trout streams the fish seem to feed avidly in the boils, while in others, I am never successful in raising a fish in boils.

However, an angler with a good basic knowledge of reading water can come to a new stream and know immediately where many good fish are located. This fundamental knowledge will prevent wasting time fishing barren water. Reading water is considered by some to be a sixth sense. These individuals write knowingly of this sense. This is nonsense. It is simply a matter of experience.

On bright days wear polaroid glasses. They will allow you

Plate 1

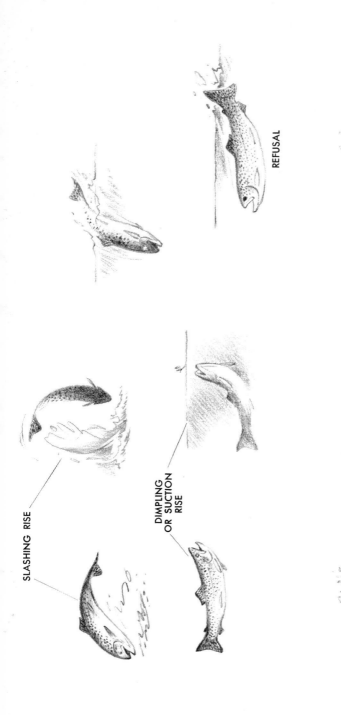

SLASHING RISE

DIMPLING
OR SUCTION
RISE

REFUSAL

LEAPING

BULGING

Fig. 13   Trout Rises

to see deep in the water. Keep your eyes open for feeding fish, both on the top and on the bottom, Fig. 13. You will very quickly learn to recognize this phenomenon. A fish may appear to be standing on his head (tailing) when he is feeding on the bottom. Feeding on nymphs, he may swirl around in the middle layers or bulge his back (bulging rises) when taking them near the surface. Then, there are the round rings (suction rises) on the surface, produced by trout deliberately on floating mayflies. Splashing or slashing rises are caused by trout coming all the way out of the water, sometimes making a complete arc, and taking the fly on the way into the water. The refusal rise is the most frustrating. A trout will be seen coming up for a dry fly and then deliberately turn and head back down just before he should have taken the fly. Change to a smaller fly and he usually will take it.

Many times it is difficult to tell the difference between a suction rise on the surface and a bulging rise from a trout feeding close to the surface. How many times have I fished a dry fly on top when I should have used a wet fly just under the surface.

Study streams at all water levels, especially during low, clear water when hidden ledges and pockets can be clearly seen. Some anglers draw maps of the streams on which they mark the topography and prevalent conditions. Most of us commit these facts to memory.

Fishing for any species of trout or salmon is seldom very good when water is rising. This is true for a rise due to rain, melting snow or water suddenly released from a dam. Fishing is usually excellent when water is falling. I have had good fishing on streams in flood as long as the water was falling.

Fish occupy three types of water: resting or holding water, feeding water and passage water. Fish occupy passage water only transiently while traveling on migration or going to and

from holding water. In the case of trout, holding and feeding water are frequently one and the same thing.

Fish, like humans, must seek out dining rooms to obtain their food. Fish dining rooms are located where converging currents bring food.

A stream may be broken into component parts, no matter what its size.

## OUTLINE OF STREAM COMPONENTS

A.  Riffles and rapids
B.  Obvious pools (oval, curved and cut-bank)
    1.  Head of pool
    2.  Middle
    3.  Tail, break and slick
C.  Deflectors
D.  Straight section of stream (a reach)
    1.  Undercut banks
    2.  Sloping or shelving banks
E.  Rocks
F.  Large back-eddies
G.  Boils
H.  Whirlpools

In all of the plates the water is flowing toward you.

## RIFFLES AND RAPIDS

Any discussion of water reading should first clearly define a riffle. Plate 5 shows a typical large, shallow riffle; likewise the right side of the island, Plate 14. A riffle is a fast-moving portion of a stream with many waves. These waves are formed by boulders in the bottom of the stream. Many times rocks protrude above the surface of the water. A riffle may be likened to a slow rapid. Many riffles containing fish are fast enough to be

considered rapids, Plates 6 and 7, Fig. 22. I am constantly
amazed to find fish feeding in such water. The secret lies in
the ability of the fish to seek out and lie in slow water behind
rocks and, less often, in front of rocks. Some riffles lead into
pools, Plate 2, Fig. 17, and some out, Plate 3, Fig. 19. Whether
they lead in or out they may contain trout if not too fast.


## POOLS

Typical pools, Plate 2, 3 and 4, Fig. 17, 19 and 20, have a
riffle or a rapid at the head. Some even have waterfalls. As the
riffle or rapid flows into the pool the current gradually slows.
The center of the pool contains slow, deep water. The tail-end,
or final third, usually has a shelving bottom that gradually
shallows until it forms a lip or break. This can be likened to
slowly pouring water out of a cup. Where the water flows over
the rim of the cup is the break and immediately below this is
a short stretch of smooth, fast water, the slick, followed by the
riffle. Plate 3, Fig. 19. These are the component parts. Trout
have definite areas that they seek out at various times of the
day and season.

Oval pools are scarce and, for the most part, are found on
small streams, frequently made by men or beavers. Plate 1,
Fig. 17, shows the upper two thirds of an oval pool in a remote,
small stream in Canada. The usual pool in a trout stream or
river is a pool with a curve in it.

Now to locate the fish. The last third of the riffle, leading
into a pool, is a favorite feeding place. If the current is not
too fast, the entire riffle may contain fish. If there are enough
large rocks or boulders in a riffle this may even be a resting
area.

The constant movement of small stones and gravel in a riffle
dislodges nymphs and other insect larvae and the current
brings them down to the waiting fish. Nymphs live in riffles

because of the relative increase in water oxygenation and abundance of their food. Trout seek out riffles during dusk of the summer months. In the spring they may be found all day feeding in these areas. On sunny days, early in the spring, when water is cold and murky, trout seek out slow and shallow riffles that they would never go near in the latter part of the season. The warmth of the sun on the water and the better visibility is a popular theory for this phenomenon.

As the riffle enters the pool, there will be noted a slow current at the side, Plate 1, Fig. 18; Plate 2, Fig. 17. Where the swift and slow currents come together, food collects and there the fish are found. This is one of the most likely places to find big, feeding fish. Here, the water is usually deep enough for large fish to sink down, hide and watch the surface for insects.

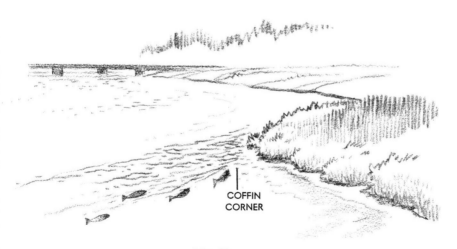

COFFIN
CORNER

Fig. 18

The fisherman who looks carefully will note that the fast and slow water will frequently form a point similar to the apex of a triangle just as the riffle breaks in the pool, Plate 1, Fig. 18; Plate 2, Fig. 17 at H. Mr. Biddle used to refer to this as 'coffin

corner.' Here, if it is deep enough, there is a tremendous collection of food and that is where the big ones frequently lie.

Many pools contain whirlpools and big boils and, in some streams, the fish feed avidly in the boils but seldom in whirlpools.

The deep, middle portion of a pool is seldom productive for fly fishermen, Plate 3, Fig. 19. Here, fish rest or hold, usually at the bottom. Occasionally, during a big hatch of caddis or stonefly, big fish come from the bottom and deliberately take a fly. Unless this rare phenomenon is occurring don't bother with this section of the pool.

At the tail-end of the pool in the region of the break, is a favorite spot for steelhead or salmon to lie, Plate 3, Fig. 19. This is also the location of many spawning beds and spawned-out fish. If there are rocks, boulders or other obstructions, trout also like to lie, rest and feed here. The corners of these areas are favorite locations for trout, providing it is deep enough and there is current.

## CUT-BANK POOLS

The inside curve of a cut-bank pool is usually shallow and gradually becomes deeper until it becomes a sheer bank or cut-bank, Plate 4, Fig. 20. This sheer bank is formed by water erosion. Everything written about curved pools holds for cut-bank pools with the exception that fish tend to lie and feed in against the cut-bank the entire length of the pool. This is particularly true of anadromous fish. (Fish that go to sea when 6-8 inches long and return as adults.)

## DEFLECTORS

Deflectors produce some of the best fishing water in a stream. An example is the log that extends out from the bank,

Plate 3, Fig. 19. Fish will rest behind this log and occasionally in front, enjoying the shade, concealment and reduced current. At the tip of the farthest log there will be noted a definite change in the main current. This illustrates the principle of a joining of fast and slow current. Here, fish may be both resting and feeding. The angler must be alert for the deflector effect. At times, deflectors will be noted to consist of rocks, stumps or branches which jut out into a stream, Plate 11. Very large deflectors frequently produce curced pools, curved riffles and eddies.

## BACK-EDDIES

Back-eddies, found in all types of pools, are an area of reverse current produced by a fast main current striking the bank at such an angle as to deflect it backwards, Plate 3, Fig. 19. They are ideal collecting areas for food and most trout find them excellent dinner tables. Unfortunately, back-eddies, whirlpools and boils do not photograph well; they must be seen under actual stream conditions to be appreciated.

## SHADED AREAS

Trout are particularly aware of shaded areas in a stream, Plates 11 and 12, Fig. 25, as a place to hide from birds of prey and as a ready source of insects dropping from the branches and overhanging grass. They will inhabit much shallower water where there is shade. This rule applies primarily to resident trout and not as much to sea-run fish. During the periods of big fly hatches they frequently seem to wait under the shade from branches of trees for the various flies to fall off into the water.

## UNDERCUT BANKS

Many streams are deep and straight with undercut banks, Plate 10, Fig. 24. The water next to the bank may be as deep as six feet and extend in under the bank six to twelve inches. There is usually grass hanging over the water. However, the bank of a stream may actually be a moss bed, Plate 13, Fig. 26, extending into the stream, as is so typical of Silver Creek in Idaho. Trout lie under these banks resting and feeding. They will feed on insects within inches of their resting place or they may swim out and feed in the main current.

## LEDGES

Sea-run fish and trout love to lie near sunken ledges. Unfortunately, these ledges are frequently not visible to the angler on the first visits to the stream. The resident angler has a distinct advantage over the visitor in that he can examine the terrain during low water.

## TRIBUTARIES

On any stream, be on the lookout for smaller streams flowing into the mainstream. If there is sufficient flow, fish are found lying above and below the mouth of the stream. A stream of sufficient size to constitute a spawning stream should be examined carefully by the angler for sea-run fish at its mouth. These fish collect in bunches at such locations in preparation for their final dash to the spawning bed.

At times of high, muddy water these small feeder streams may be the only place that the fisherman can fish his fly. They will form areas of clear water in the muddy water of the main stream.

## ISLANDS

Many large streams have islands scattered along their courses. The more difficult the island is to reach the better is the fishing. John Q. Public does not like to walk or wade in difficult places. Remember, trying to wade to an island is a dandy way to drown. Wear an adequate life preserver or don't fish islands. Plate 14, Fig. 27 illustrates a large island. There are large rocks on the left side just opposite the large tree. Behind these are some real hot spots. Observe carefully the water extending behind the island. The current from each side of the island gradually comes together and extends downstream at least 100 feet. In this location I have caught many of my biggest trout. This is a natural banquet hall.

## HIDDEN POOLS

Most of the time we read water from the top down. Plate 7 appears as a simple, flat piece of water. We look at the bottom first. Lo! There is a 75-foot-long pool about six feet in depth.

On some slow, meandering rivers, providing the water is clear, careful scrutiny of the bottom will soon reveal pools with typical deflectors, rocks, etc. With this knowledge the angler presents his fly properly.

Brown trout occupy the same location as rainbow, but brown trout prefer slower-moving streams. Many brown trout streams require bottom reading.

I begin to sense a feeling of impatience. Do not despair. In the chapter on fishing techniques we will retrace our steps and fish all the water that I have described. My! The fish we'll catch!

# CHAPTER 5

## *Entomology*

Here are the water-bred insects fly fishermen need to know:

### *Aquatic Insects*

| Common Name | Latin Name |
|---|---|
| Mayfly | Ephemeroptera |
| Caddis fly | Trichoptera |
| Stonefly | Plecoptera |
| True fly (Midges) | Diptera |
| Dragonfly | Odonata |

Here are the land-bred insects fly fishermen should know:

### *Terrestrial Insects*

| Common Name | Latin Name |
|---|---|
| Grasshopper | Orthoptera |
| Bee and ant | Hymenoptera |
| Beetle | Coleoptera |
| True fly | Diptera |
| Moth | Lepidoptera |

A fly fisherman will have great difficulty differentiating the three most important aquatic flies: mayfly, caddis fly and stonefly, Fig. 14. All three have two sets of wings. Most mayflies have only a rudimentary second pair. While at rest the mayfly holds its wings in a vertical position.

Identifying either the caddis fly or the stone fly is not difficult. The caddis, when at rest, holds its wings over its body

34

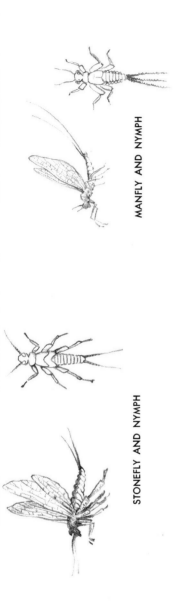

MANFLY AND NYMPH

STONEFLY AND NYMPH

MIDGE

CADDIS AND CASED LARVA

CADDIS AND STONEFLY AT REST

Fig. 14   Natural Flies and Nymphs

like a peaked roof. The stone fly wings are folded flat over the body.

## Mayflies

The mayfly deserves first attention. While true flies, mostly tiny, inconspicuous kinds, are of primary importance as trout food, the mayfly is most commonly noticed by anglers. This insect goes through four stages in its life cycle. The nymph hatches from the egg, transforms after attaining full growth to the Dun and finally to the Spinner.

In the nymph stage, Fig. 14, the insect is entirely aquatic. It undergoes several changes of skin before it reaches the final stage and floats or swims to the surface to finally break out of its last nymphal skin to the Dun. An erratic path may be followed when the mature nymph floats or swims upward; it may go up and down, somewhat like an elevator, before it finally floats on the surface.

As a nymph, the mayfly is an even more important source of food than as a floating fly. Trout spend most of their time foraging on the bottom for this kind of food. Larvae of tiny true flies, caddis flies and the nymphs of mayflies make up the majority of this food. Stone fly nymphs comprise a smaller part of the food supply.

Mayfly nymphs are commonly found under and around rocks. The nymphs of the giant mayfly, commonly referred to in the adult stage as Drakes, occupy areas of silt but not of compact sand or mud. Most mayfly nymphs, however, are found in rocky areas. Their color varies with the color of the stream bottom. The commonest colors are dark brown backs and brown, olive-green or yellow bellies.

Some nymphs crawl from place to place, some swim part of the time and others burrow in silt or loose sand.

For years I was confused about flat and round-bodied mayfly

nymphs. They both hatch into mayflies. Most flat-bodied nymphs live around or under rocks in relatively fast water and have the ability to crawl. Most round-bodied nymphs live in silt or slow-water situations; some of these can actually swim to new locations.

The nymphal stage of mayflies may last for several months, in some cases for as long as two years; most nymphs transform to adults in three to six months. They undergo several changes of skin before they emerge from the water. Trout feeding on the bottom for nymphs, at times, appear to be standing on their heads (tailing) as they nudge around the rocks and gravel. When this condition exists the fisherman should use a deeply sunk nymphy fly or nymph.

How many times have I fished over large swirls on the surface to no avail only to realize that I was fishing over trout taking nymphs floating close to the surface. Under these conditions the dry fly is worthless. A nymph sunk one or two feet beneath the surface is more logical. Shortly after the nymph arrives at the surface the skin splits open and the first fly stage, or Dun, struggles out to ride the discarded skin as a raft. Duns, at this stage, are very weak fliers. They are called Duns because their wings have a smoky dull appearance. The mayfly is most succulent and nutritious at this stage. Trout prefer this form and feed avidly. When feeding on Duns they rise slowly and deliberately suck in the fly. This produces characteristic suction rings on the water. Duns usually fly directly up into the air and land in bushes and trees where they again shed their skin and transform to the final Spinner stage.

The angler can tell a Dun hatch simply by watching these insects fly slowly up into the air. When the fly returns to the water it is no longer a Dun but a glistening Spinner. Some refer to the mayfly egg-laying process as "spinning her eggs," hence the term Spinner.

Spinners and Duns look very much alike to the untrained

eye; however, there is usually a change in color. The Spinner's body and wings are brighter, the belly lighter in color and the dark markings on the back are sharper in contrast. When the Dun sits on the water half of the body is curled off of the surface. In contrast, in one group of mayflies, the Spinner floats flat on the water since she must extend her body full-length to utilize the current to help strip or spin the hundreds of eggs from her two egg sacs.

The Spinner of other mayflies may drop her eggs in flight or even crawl under the surface and lay them on a submerged rock or stick. Before laying her eggs, the female Spinner mates in the air with a male Spinner usually over land. Shortly after mating, the male dies and his body usually falls on the land. The ripe female Spinner then flies down, deposits some eggs, quickly rises, lands in another location and repeats the process. Her time on the water is sometimes only momentary. Trout must rise quickly to catch the fly. This accounts for the slashing rises with the fish frequently coming entirely out of the water.

Finally, the female Spinner falls to the surface, often with her wings outstretched. Anglers refer to such a female as a spentwing Spinner. Spentwing dry flies, with wings tied in a horizontal position, represent this fly. The spentwing Spinner contains little nutrition though trout may feed widely on them at times.

Big hatches of mayflies usually do not occur until the water temperature reaches about 52°. However, I have seen good hatches appear with snow falling and the water temperature in the 40's. In my experience these hatches consist of small mayflies. In the Pacific Northwest they appear at any time during the winter months. I have never seen them, though, when there was ice in the water.

## Caddis Flies (Sedges)

The caddis fly and its larva is just as important or more important on some streams than the mayfly. It varies in size from tiny to giant flies two inches in wing span. The caddis larva is best described as a round grub or creeper in a case. It may be pale yellow, white or blue-green in color. Shortly after it hatches from the egg, the caddis immediately starts the construction of a suitable cage or house. The type of case is typical of a specific group of these flies, and every member of that group will build a case of approximately the same material and pattern so that caddis worms of the same species are easily identified. Some employ gravel, some vegetable matter, some a combination of both, binding them and cementing them together with a silken substance which the worm excretes. The cases are of various shapes, most often cylindrical or tapered. Some species live on the sides of rocks, behind screens of brush and aquatic plants; nets that trap their food supply. Others drag their cases as they crawl over the bottom of the stream. The familiar "periwinkle," known to all fishermen, is one of the crawling variety. The case protects it from predatory stonefly and dragonfly nymphs. Trout eat the caddis worm, case and all, and have no difficulty expelling the empty cases.

When the caddis worm reaches maturity it seals up the front end of its case and develops into the pupal stage and acquires wing cases. It awakens from the period of dormancy, tears open the sealed end and emerges, swathed in a thin membrane. The insect swims to the surface, with middle legs free of the sheath, the sheath is broken and the winged caddis takes flight.

After arriving at the winged stage, the caddis fly does not change in structure, as does the mayfly, and is ready for mating and egg-laying at once.

I have seen caddis flies emerging only once. This was in the

summer at late dusk. They apparently hatch out during the night. Probably all caddis flies consume water and perhaps other liquids with their sucking-type mouth parts. For this reason, the adult caddis, unlike the mayfly, may live for a matter of weeks. They often fly in swarms, usually close to the surface of the water. At sunset they may swarm over the tips of the trees, forming a dancing halo. They mate in mid-air in a fashion somewhat similar to mayflies.

The various species of caddis use different methods of egg laying. Some females skim along the surface, using the water film to strip eggs from their bodies. They appear to be fluttering along the water. In British Columbia these are known as "traveling sedges." Other kinds drop to the water's surface, rise up in the air, again and again, in a fashion similar to the mayfly Spinner. Still other caddis flies dive to the surface from the air and swim down to lay their eggs under water. Some caddis flies crawl down on the sides of rocks, sticks, etc., and deposit their eggs.

### STONEFLY

#### (Salmon Fly, Willow Fly)

The stonefly is to trout what filet mignon is to man. This was recognized by Sir Charles Cotton in his addition to Isaac Walton's "The Compleat Anglers," three centuries ago.

I have caught trout, during the time of the salmon fly, so gorged that the flies were literally hanging out of their mouths. The term 'salmon fly' is applied to the large two-inch stonefly that appears on Eastern Oregon streams during the spring salmon runs.

The stonefly nymph lives among the rocks and boulders in relatively fast water. It may be a vegetarian or a carnivore. The

carnivorous species feed with great gusto on the nymphs of the mayfly and on larvae of caddis flies and midges.

Stonefly nymphs look like mayfly nymphs. Mayfly nymph feet have a single claw while stoneflies have a pair of them. Virtually all mayfly nymphs have gills extending out from the sides of their abdomens while those of the stonefly extend from the thorax. The life span under water ranges from one to three years. Stoneflies do not undergo a pupal stage, as do the caddis. Neither do they molt after arriving at wing stage. The change from nymph to winged, apart from acquiring wings, is slight. The mature nymph crawls up a rock, stick, etc., sheds its nymphal skin and emerges as an adult fly. The stonefly nymph, like the caddis, emerges primarily at night. Its life span is about the same as the caddis. They mate on the limbs of trees, other objects or on the ground. The female most often deposits eggs while flying. These eggs may be deposited as a single egg-mass or released in small groups; they sink rapidly to the bottom.

### Other Aquatic Insects

The Dobson fly and its nymph, the hellgramite, are both attractive food to trout. The nymph is located in the same region as the stonefly. It is never found in great numbers in the West, consequently, is not a major source of food.

The dragonfly and its nymphs find their way occasionally into a trout stomach but are of little importance.

### Midges, Blackflies and Punkies

### (Aquatic Diptera)

Diptera, or true flies, are both aquatic and non-aquatic. The non-aquatic are frequently blown into the water and taken by

trout. The mosquito, although aquatic, has its life cycle in stagnant pools, tin cans, etc., and by most fishermen is considered to be a terrestrial insect. It is not an important source of food, although there is a famous fly called the Mosquito.

The aquatic diptera in the larval stage are the most important source of trout food in most streams and all lakes. The most important source! This statement by my consulting fish biologists really astounds me. These flies consist mainly of midges, tiny blackflies and punkies, or no-see-ums. When one considers that there have been estimated to be one to two hundreds pounds of insect life per acre of fertile trout stream there must be an amazing number of diptera larvae on the stream bottom. Because of their size, they are not noticed by fishermen as they hatch. Their relative importance varies from stream to stream. In some, midges are most important, while in others, the blackflies or punkies. There are also some streams in which diptera are not as important as the mayfly, caddis or stonefly. These streams are usually soft water and low in lime content, hence not very fertile.

English fly fishermen call the midge hatch 'the curse.' This tiny fly hatches in veritable swarms. During such a hatch trout rise all over a pool. The largest rise of feeding fish I have ever seen has been to a midge hatch at dusk. The midges we commonly associate with these swarms are of a type called non-biting midges. The adult is easily recognized because of its tiny size. There is only one pair of wings; the hind pair being reduced to slender, club-shaped, balancing organs. The life cycle consists of the usual egg, larva, pupal and adult stages. Midge larvae are most abundant in the shallow water areas of lakes, ponds and streams, favored by a heavy growth of aquatic plants. However, in such areas, they are preyed upon more heavily by large insects and fish so that more adult midges may actually emerge from the deeper regions. Like

mayflies they do not like sand. The bottom dwellers are found on soft, mucky bottoms; the others, where there is much vegetation such as water weeds, cattails, grasses, etc. The life history may vary considerably; in warm water there may be a number of generations a year, whereas the same species in a cold lake may require a year or more for emergence.

Midges in the adult stage must be a very tasty dish to produce such tremendous rises of trout.

Years ago, Edward Hewitt wondered why trout fed so voraciously at times on floating insects. Being an excellent organic chemist, he subjected all types of common aquatic insects to chemical analysis. He found them to be an amazing source of high-protein, high-energy food.

### Land-Bred or Terrestrial Insects

During the warm months of the spring, summer and fall, land-bred insects become more important floating feed for trout.

During grasshopper time, walk in the high grass close to the bank of a stream. This old trick will cause them to jump in the water. Then, fish that section of the stream with a hopper fly. You have, in a sense, created your own hatch.

Fly fishermen on the La Torte River in Pennsylvania await eagerly the Japanese beetle invasion, so cursed by the farmers. They tie a special fly to imitate this insect. When the beetle is on the water, this is the insect that the trout prefer above all.

There must be something extra tasty about the flying ant. On trout streams west of the Cascades in Oregon some of the best fly fishing can be had with the imitation in late April and early May. They seem to prefer this fly partially sunk.

One evening in August I found my favorite Washington cut-throat stream covered with brown moths. I have never seen

this before or since. Fortunately, the fish thought my #10 orange caddis was the same as the moth. I enjoyed a remarkable evening's fishing.

Always keep your eyes open for terrestrials. Who knows, you may run into a swarm of locusts, the seventeen-year type or others. When this occurs in our streams we frequently get tired releasing fish. Terrestrials . . . the fish and I both love them!!

I usually open the stomach of the first trout I catch and examine the contents for predominant nymphs or flies. This is best done by the use of the white china cup and a little water. However, don't rely entirely on this method. Many times a trout's stomach will be gorged with a certain nymph but actually he may have decided to change his bill-of-fare and feed on dry flies. If you try to present to him the nymph found in his stomach he may ignore it completely.

Until recently, preservation of flies in their natural colors for any long period of time was impossible. The colors faded rapidly in the common preserving solutions made of alcohol, formaldehyde, etc. Now, with the advent of new preserving solutions invented by the Armed Forces Institute of Pathology, this is no longer true.

Formula:
    Sodium Phosphate Monobasic 8.9 gm.
    Sodium Phosphate Dibasic 11.3 gm.
    Formaldehyde solution (40%) 95 cc.
    Distilled Water Q.S. ad 190 cc.

Divide this solution in half. Mark them solutions one and two. To solution two, add sodium hydrosulfite to an extent of 0.5%. As soon as a specimen is captured place it in solution one. The specimen will lose most of its color. Allow it to remain in solution one for 3 to 7 days then transfer specimen to

solution two. This is the final solution in which the specimen will be kept permanently. Solution two restores the natural color to the specimen. The time that the specimen remains in solution one varies. Human tissue must remain for at least two weeks.

# CHAPTER 6

## *Flies*

More has been written about flies than any other part of fly fishing. This preoccupation with flies has prevented many from becoming skillful. Edward Hewitt emphasized that <u>only a few fly patterns are necessary to catch the majority of feeding trout.</u> Flies may be roughly divided into wet and dry. These, in turn, may be classified as imitators, impressionists and attractors.

Imitators are exact reproductions of the actual insect larvae or minnow. They are usually made of various plastics and solid materials. In the water they only give off two or three primary colors. The consensus of opinion is that they are worthless.

Most of the flies anglers use are impressionists. They give the fish the impression of the insect. They are created of natural substances, mainly feathers and fur blended together. An impressionist fly gives off many tiny color waves of various shades and intensity. These blend together to give the same final subtle color effect as produced by the natural fly. A fish rising to a natural fly usually does not stop and inspect it; merely has a momentary impression and seizes it.

The relative importance of size, color and form is debatable. I feel that size is most important, then color, then form.

Attractor flies are tied of natural material and usually do not imitate any known insect. They are a combination of bright colors that attract and even anger fish. The Royal Coachman is the most famous and probably the greatest, especially when there is no insect hatch on the water. The bulk of the flies used for anadromous fish are attractors.

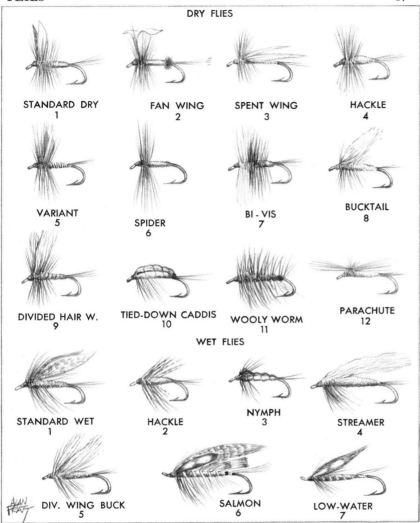

Fig. 15  Flies

From this point on we will disregard imitators and only be concerned with impressionists and attractors.

Dry flies are fished on top of the water and wet flies beneath. The construction is guided by this. However, a dry fly may be used as a wet fly and vice versa. Figure 15 depicts most of the

varieties of wet and dry fly. A quick appraisal reveals the standard dry fly has upright wings and a round hackle while the standard wet fly has a slanting wing and a flat hackle. Most of these flies are tied to represent primarily impressionist May and Caddis flies. I use very few standard wet flies. In their place I find most dry flies work as well.

The beginning fly fisherman, when confronted with a catalogue from one of the stores that specializes in flies, becomes hopelessly confused. Figure 15 is an attempt to bring order out of confusion.

1. *Standard divided-wing dry fly:* See previous description.

2. *Fan-wing:* A dry fly with large wings; the emphasis is on the wings. This fly probably represents a spent Spinner and they are popular on the East Coast.

3. *Spent-wing:* Represents a spent Spinner. The wings are usually tied with hackle tips. The emphasis is again on the wings.

4. *Hackle fly:* My favorite; exactly like the standard dry fly except without wings. Like many other fishermen I do not feel the wings contribute anything but looks to a low or clear water dry fly. I especially like these because they are easier to tie.

5. *Variant:* A fly with large hackles, out of proportion to the wing and hook. These flies supposedly represent a high-floating Dun.

6. *Spider:* Similar to a variant only without wings. The hackles are even larger in proportion to the hook.

7. *Bivisible:* Invented by the late Edward Hewitt. Good for both high and low water conditions; floats well in rough water; bivisible because the white front hackle makes it visible to the fisherman as well as the fish. The hackle extends the entire length of the hook; this is referred to as Palmar-tied. Many claim brown and gray bivisible in various sizes is the only fly necessary to catch trout on a dry fly. This fly works equally well as a wet fly.

8. *Bucktail:* Wing made of bucktail. These represent large Caddis and Stone flies. When these flies are on the water they work well in high or low water conditions. This is a dual-purpose fly. When fished wet as a streamer fly it represents minnows as well as Caddis and Stone flies. The illustration is tied with dry fly fishing in mind.

9. *Divided hair-wing or wulff type fly:* My favorite high or rough water dry fly. The bucktail or hair-wing gives this fly excellent floating characteristics. Fished wet and pulled against the current, wings pulsate, giving an enticing action. This type is primarily for dry fly fishing.

10. *Tied-down-bucktail:* Popularly referred to as a tied down Caddis. For some reason, at times more effective than a regular bucktail. When fished wet looks like a Caddis nymph.

11. *Woolly worm:* A Palmar-tied fly on a long shank hook, tied to represent a caterpillar. Fished wet, I suspect it also represents a Stone fly nymph. Popular in Colorado and Montana streams; also works well on the West Coast.

12. *Parachute fly:* Figure 16. The variety I prefer perfected by Lloyd Byerly of Portland, Oregon. He has invented a simple method of tying this fly; excellent floater. Lloyd feels that trout fished over heavily become accustomed to the standard dry fly and a different-appearing fly will entice them when standards will not. All standard patterns may be tied as parachute flies. The post in the center is usually tied with white calf tail which enhances visibility. Wet, it looks like a nymph. They are excellent in both high and low water. I use this fly for about 60% of my dry fly fishing.

## Wet Flies

1. *Standard wet fly:* See previous description.

2. *Hackle fly:* Fly similar to dry fly shown under dry flies except the hackles are frequently tied with soft hen hackles

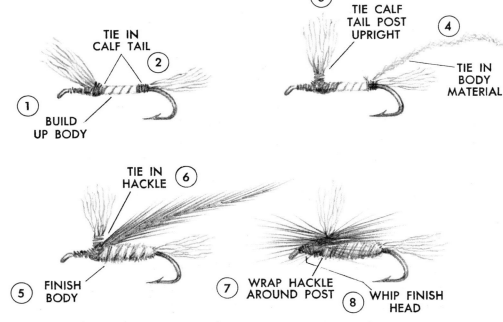

Fig. 16   Buszek's Parachute (by Byerly)

instead of gamecock hackles. Hackles usually slant backwards. You will frequently hear the term nymph fly used. These are finely-tied hackle flies and were popularized in this country by James Leisenring.

3. *Nymphs:* This is the closest to an actual imitation. The blending of natural materials in its construction prevents it from being classified as a true imitator. There is a controversy among experts in this field as to which represents the natural nymph the best, the nymph fly or the nymph.

4. *Streamer:* Similar to classic wet fly, only with longer wings. Represents minnows, young trout and salmon. Many are tied as attractor flies. Wings may be tied with feathers, bucktail or maribou.

5. *Divided-wing bucktail:* Popular on Rogue River for sum-

mer steelhead; usually tied without hackles; wing slants back more than the wulff-type dry fly; usually tied as attractor flies.

6. *Classic English salmon fly; Heavy water variety:* These are complex-tied flies for Atlantic salmon. When tied in proper patterns, work equally well for steelhead.

7. *Classic English salmon fly; low water variety:* Similar to the classic English heavy water variety except lightly tied.

## Fly Selection

Selection of patterns should be guided by the locality one desires to fish. A good native fly fisherman or local fly shop can be of inestimable help in fly selection. A cardinal point to remember: a few patterns of various sizes are preferable to a great many patterns all of the same size.

It is possible to have a selection of flies which will catch the majority of feeding trout throughout the entire United States. In selecting this list I have kept in mind high and low water conditions or, expressed in another manner, rough and clear water. Remember, heavily tied flies for heavy water, lightly tied flies for clear water. Any of the flies described under the column as clear-water flies may be tied with hair wings and heavy hackle and become heavy water flies.

## Dry Flies

### (Clear Water)

*Quill-Gordon—18, 14, 10; smokey gray
*Adams—18, 14, 10; gray-brown
*Light Cahill—18, 14, 10; light, yellow-brown
March Brown—14, 10; brown
*Red upright—14, 19; red-brown
Olive Dun—14, 10; olive
Black Gnat—14, 10; black
*Brown Spider—12

The three patterns selected in size 18—Quill Gordon, Adams and Light Cahill—should be tied as hackle flies without wings. These represent midges in this size. The flies marked with an asterisk (*) are in my opinion the most essential patterns for dry-fly fishing. If limited to one size, choose #14.

## Dry Flies

### (Heavy Water)

*Bucktail Royal Coachman—12; red and white
*Irresistible—12; gray-brown
*Muddler Minnow—10; brown
 Gray Wulff—12; gray
 White Wulff—12; white

## Nymphs and Nymph Flies

*Gray Nymph—10, 14; gray
*Ed Burke—12, 14; black
*Birdstone Salmon fly nymph—8; brown with orange overtones
*Atherton Medium—12, 14; gray brown
*Olive May fly nymph—12, 14; olive

## Streamer Flies

*Bucktail Royal Coachman—10, 8
*Mickey Finn—10, 8; orange and red
*Gray Ghost—10, 8; gray
 Black-nosed Dase—10, 8
 Rainbow—10, 8

If limited to one size choose #10.

## Choosing the Proper Fly

The choice of the proper dry fly is quite simple. Select the fly from your box which comes closest to the size, color and shape that appears (or should appear) on the water.

Wet fly fishing is more demanding in its fly requirements. A knowledge of local stream entomology is a tremendous help. A few minutes spent kicking rocks will help decide the proper nymph or wet fly.

Streamer fly fishing will always be a trial and error technique, especially with attractor streamers which make up 80% of all streamer fishing. Local lore is of paramount importance. The Royal Coachman seems to work everywhere.

## Leader Selection

The size of the fly you select and the condition of the water determine the size of your leader. Much has been written about leader color. I have never noted any difference between natural monofilament or gut and the stained variety, as far as the number of fish caught. The big factor is the size of gut.

Fine, long leaders for clear, low water and small flies; coarser leaders and larger flies for rough and colored water.

The shortest leaders I ever use are nine feet and the longest about twelve feet. Some nymph fishermen use leaders as long as twenty feet. In dry and wet fly fishing the commonest size is a 4X—nine foot leader for size 14 and 12 flies; 5X for size 16 and midges; 2X for size 8 and 6 wet flies.

I have yet to meet a skillful fly fisherman who, at some time or other, did not tie his own flies. I take a fly tying kit with me on extended fishing trips; especially into new country. Being able to tie the right fly has many times meant the difference between the proper fly and fish and no fish. Many fly tiers claim that tying their own flies saves money, but the

amount of supplies and equipment that one must have on hand balances out any saving. The main reason for fly tying is to experiment and to have flies tied according to your preference.

There is only one way of beating the cost of flies . . . that is to buy cheap flies. Many fly shops have sales during the year. I watch for these, as my wife does, for bargains in the local supermarket. These flies are well-tied flies that are overstocked or simply have not been popular. However, a great many are inexpensive Japanese imports. The latter must be selected with great care. First, test the hook for brittleness and softness. Then pull on the hackles and wings. If they pass these tests then buy. The next step is proper clipping. Most of these flies are too bushy and the hackles are too soft. There is nothing you can do about the softness of the hackles except apply a good fly dope. Clipping out at least two thirds of the hackle will result in a peculiar appearing fly but will catch fish as well as the most expensive fly. The addition of a drop of clear nail polish to the head of these cheap imports is a wise precaution.

Flies are fascinating and fun to experiment with, but they are third in importance to reading water and proper fly presentation. In your fishing career if you will emphasize these two factors you will catch many more fish than the man who emphasize flies and fly patterns.

# CHAPTER 7

## *Wading*

Ten percent of the fishermen are supposed to catch ninety percent of the fish. Ninety percent of the fishermen wade when they should not. There seems to be an irresistible urge for the novice to get into the water, somewhat analogous to the small boy and the mud puddle. There are three basic reasons for wading:

1. To present the fly properly. As an example, overhanging tree limbs that prevent a roll or side cast from the shore to a likely area.

2. The stream is too wide and wading is the only way the fisherman can reach a likely spot. This is the biggest cause for a fisherman mistakenly wading through good fishing water to cast to an obvious spot. Obvious fishing spots can be seen and fished by everyone, hence, usually contain few fish. The out-of-the-way pockets and riffles are especially productive; these account for the expert's success.

3. The fisherman's presence may be too obvious when he stands on the bank. An example of this is Silver Creek in Idaho. This river, when conditions are right, is a winding, slow-moving river full of moss or water plants. The water level is practically even with the soft, spongy bank. Any step can be felt by a trout for a great distance. In this situation the fisherman is also silhouetted against the sky. By wading close to the bank he is much less visible. Depending on the speed of the current, walking upstream sends vibrations only a few

feet upstream. I have hooked fish as close as six feet from me and have had them rise to a natural fly at my elbow. If you must wade, wade slowly, quietly and carefully. I have put more fish down by wading carelessly than I have ever caught.

Every fisherman should perform this experiment at least once. Go below a wading fisherman at least 100 to 200 feet. Put your head under water and listen. The racket is astounding! Downstream wading must be done in a slow, pause-and-wait fashion.

The foot work used in wading is similar to that used in boxing. The angler goes forward or retreats with one foot always advanced. Standing with both feet close together while wading is an invitation to a swim.

Wading staffs are a nuisance; however, in very fast water they can mean the difference between a wet and dry angler. A long, light aluminum ski pole with the basket removed makes a dandy wading staff. A short rope should be attached to the handle and this attached to the belt to allow the staff to hang free when fishing. I personally find a new pole every time I need one and discard it when I have finished using it. On the average big stream, one seldom uses the staff more than two or three times in a day's fishing.

Any fisherman who wades in water above his thighs and does not wear some form of life preserver is a damn fool. I too had to learn this the hard way. There are several fishing vests on the market today that incorporate a rubber bladder, which can be inflated by a $CO_2$ cartridge. Keep about a quart of air in the bladder. You know then that it does not leak and the amount of air contributes some buoyancy until you can pull the lanyard that releases the $CO_2$.

If you fish long enough, you are bound to slip and be forced to swim. Don't panic! Keep your feet down and tread water. Go with the current, bounce your feet on the bottom, if pos-

sible; at the same time, angle in toward shore. Usually it is impossible to swim back to the spot from which you started. A great deal of strength is wasted trying to do so. If you are caught in a large rapid with numerous boulders, assume a sitting position and put your feet in front of you to act as a bumper. The Navy teaches their frogmen to come through a rocky surf in this manner.

There has been a great deal of nonsense written about waders and hipboots pulling the fisherman down. Archimedes' principle disproves this. I do wear a belt around my waders. In case of a fall it helps to keep the water out and it prevents the trapping of air. Much has been said pro and con the possibility of waders trapping air and turning the luckless fisherman over to float downstream head down. It can happen! It happened to me! I was standing close to a ledge, both feet went out from under me. I went over backwards, my waders trapped air and I floated downstream upside-down. I panicked but finally managed to right myself. I stood up in about four feet of water. My partner, Bronc Choate, nearly fell in laughing.

Choice of wading equipment is a dilemma. Most use hipboots with attached rubber feet . . . preferably with felt soles. Pieces of carpet glued on with Plyabond (Goodyear) do as well.

Waist-high waders present a real problem. Stocking-foot waders with separate wading shoes are lighter, slightly easier to walk in, dry out faster and are more expensive. Once you own them they are hard to get rid of. First, the waders wear out and you still have good shoes. Then you purchase a new pair of waders and then the shoes wear out . . . this goes on endlessly!

I prefer rubberboot-foot waders. They are easier to take on and off, warmer and cheaper. During the course of the day's fishing, I like to stop and rest and remove my waders. I per-

sonally can walk in them as well as the stockingfoot waders with wading shoes.

Again, I repeat . . . DON'T wade without a life preserver! If you are unfortunate enough to get into trouble without a preserver, don't panic. Waders will not pull you under. Go with the current and all will be well. I know! I have done it both ways more than once.

## COMMON ERRORS IN FLY FISHING

1. Slurping the fly from the water because of dissatisfaction with a cast.
2. More than three false casts.
3. Over-wading.
4. Too-bushy flies.

# PART TWO

## Stream Tactics

# CHAPTER 8

## First Trip

The fundamental part of this book is finished. We will take several trips together to demonstrate practical stream tactics, in various seasons, to fish for rainbow and brown trout.

It is a lovely sunny June day. There was a heavy rain about one week ago and the stream is at its ideal, midseason water level; not high and not low.

We arrive at the oval pool Plate 2, Figure 17, at 8:00 a.m. With the exception of very hot weather late in the season I have seldom had good fishing much before 8:00 a.m. Mr. Biddle even claimed that he caught more fish around noon than at any other time.

A few Blue Duns can be seen rising from the water. Let's rig up! We will both fish dry flies with floating lines, and nine-foot 4X leaders. I will use a #14 Blue Upright and you a #14 Quill Gordon. They both represent essentially the same fly.

This pool is about 100 feet long and about 50 feet wide; a small pool. Although it is an oval pool there is no slack water in the mid-portion as there is in most oval pools. You know, oval pools occur primarily in small streams; pools in large streams usually have a curve in them.

We will start fishing at the tail of this pool and work upstream. Our first location will be on the left side of the picture, Plate 2, Fig. 17. The water is flowing from right to left. Put your first cast at about point 'A.'

The fly came down beautifully. Now bring in line as it drifts toward you. There is too much slack in your line. That's

Fig. 17   Oval Pool

Plate 2

Plate 3

better . . . you have just the right amount of slack now. Bring it in slowly, roll cast it off the water and cast it to point 'B.' Still no rise? Your next cast should place the fly just behind that rock at point 'C.'

You broke the fly off in the fish's mouth! You used too much arm in your strike! When you have a short line without much slack just use your wrist; use your arm and your wrist when you have a lot of slack line. Tie another Quill Gordon on; now, cast to point 'D' just ahead of that rock. You hooked one!! It's a beauty and it must be 16 inches long!! Reel in the slack in your hand and get the fish on your reel. Now he's going to jump! Lower the tip a bit and give him some slack. He's still on but he's getting tired; see him turn on his side? Be sure to net him head-first, otherwise he might swim out of the net.

Next, cast to point 'E' on the other side of the rock. You missed that rise! You struck too late because you did not use enough arm when you struck against all that slack line. Now try a cast to the edge of the bushes.

I'll let you decide where to make your next cast. To point 'I'? Wrong! If you do that you will have to cast over all that good water at points 'F' and 'G' and will put any fish down. Try 'F' and 'G' first and then 'I.'

I'm going to leave you now and explore a little bit. I'll be back in a few minutes. Be sure to fish 'H,' 'J,' 'K,' and 'L' in that order.

*As we fished in the preceding paragraphs we utilized the quartering upstream presentation of Chapter III, page 21, the commonest method of fishing the dry fly.*

You are now standing on the second fishing spot, Fig. 17. Notice that it has not been necessary to wade to present your fly properly. Last week I found one poor fellow standing in the

middle of this pool at point 'F' casting to the opposite shore. He did not realize that he was standing right in some of the best water. I have seen this happen time after time.

We are going to change our tactics. Put your fly in your mouth and moisten it. I know it is a dry fly but we are going to fish it as a wet one. First, cast directly below to point 'H.' Sink the fly by pulling it under and then bring it back slowly with little twitches of the rod tip in order to give the fly a swimming motion. Now, cast to 'K' and repeat the procedure. You are fishing the most productive water, namely, where the fast and slow water meet. Cast your fly in progressive stages to 'I' and 'G.' Each time your fly will swing around into the smooth water area on your side. When it finishes its swing, allow the fly to pause for at least 30 seconds or a minute. Then strip off a few feet of line and let the fly drift back a foot or two, then bring it in with little twitches.

*The above is the quartering down and across stream presentation in Chapter III, page 19. The commonest method of fishing the wet fly.*

When you started fishing this pool with a curved upstream cast you could have allowed the fly to swing around on each cast until it was quartering downstream. Then, giving an extra hard jerk, sink the fly and fish it as a wet fly.

*This is the wet-dry method with a combination of the curved upstream and the quartering downstream presentation.*

In a short pool like this it is possible to fish the entire pool, using a long line, with a downstream wet-dry method from position 2 and never use the upstream technique. Cast first to the nearest water, where the fast and slow water meet, as shown

in points 'H' and 'F,' then cast to the farthest waters. Don't overfish the water; most people do!

If, while fishing the dry fly in the wet fashion, you should see a trout rise to a natural fly, bring your fly in, blot it with a dry handkerchief, then re-apply mucilin. Voila! You are again ready to cast a dry fly.

Having decimated this pool of its fish population, let us now proceed to the curved pool, Plate 3.

## CURVED POOL AND DEFLECTOR

The section of river depicted in Plate 3, Fig. 19, reveals two basic pools. We are looking upstream and the water is flowing toward us. The pool at our feet is produced by two sunken logs, extending diagonally out into the current, and is a beautiful example of a pool formed by a deflector. The pool above this where the big log has fallen into the water is a good example of a large, curved pool.

We will first fish the deflector pool. Here is a situation we must wade to fish properly. We will walk directly out about six feet from where we are now standing and the picture was taken; just far enough to clear the brush with our back cast. The water here is just below our knees.

Start casting at 'A,' then cast to 'B' near the end of the log, next to 'C' and then in the sequence as indicated by the letters to cover the entire water. Don't forget to bring in the slack as your fly drifts back to you.

A large trout just rose to your fly and turned back before taking it. Why? You have the correct pattern but it is too large. Change from a #12 Blue Upright to a #14 and try again. You've hooked a beauty!

He is tired now and on his side; bring him gently up to you. Reach down with your cupped hand and lift up under his belly. Now there is no net and line to untangle. Just take

Fig. 19   Curve and Reflector Pool

the hook out and gently return him. Once you have a firm grasp on a trout's belly he usually stops struggling. Most of the truly skillful trout fishermen I have known did not bother with a net. When they land a fish they either catch it in their hands or, if too large, beach it.

Let's climb back on the bank and go up to the actual curved pool. You will see pools like this many times. It is big and we can waste a lot of time fishing non-productive water. Looking up from the deflector logs there is a long rapids. It looks fishable in the picture, but the water is too fast and too shallow. There is not enough protection for either rainbow or brown trout. Just above this is the region of the break, Fig. 19; sometimes in the evening you will find native trout in this location. It is also one that sea-run fish, such as salmon, steelhead and cut-throat trout like to lie in and, if proper gravel is present, it is the commonest spawning area.

We could fish up the left side of the pool, fishing primarily between the fast and smooth water. However, this is the most obvious and exactly the same situation we encountered in the last pool. Consequently, we are going to find two stout poles and wade across to the other side. We will start just in front of us and go directly across. Check your life vest and let's go!

From the break on up, the water to the right is about eight feet deep. We are not going to find a location for trout until we reach a small pocket of reverse current or back-eddy water. This is located at point 'H.' This is a spot often neglected by the average fisherman. Here are big fish. The water is still deep but there is a natural collecting place for food. How are we going to approach this? The bank is steep. We will walk to fishing point 2 located 6 feet downstream from the back-eddy. Another location is fishing point 3 on top of the bank. We could use point 3 if the bank is too steep to stand on. This is the least preferable location because of the difficulty of pre-

senting the fly and the possibility of the trout seeing us silhouetted against the sky.

You see those tiny flies starting to appear on the water? We
are about to experience a midge hatch. It is about the right
time of the evening for one to appear. We'll either have tremendous fishing or be completely frustrated. The English call
such a hatch. 'The Curse.' Size and color are paramount in
fishing a midge hatch. A #20 hook will do for the size. We
will ascertain the color by dipping a few midges from the water.
They are a dark gray-blue Midge. Unless one can reasonably
match the color, as well as the size, few fish will be hooked.
We must now change our leader. We can do two things; put on
nine-foot 5X leader or tie a 5X tippet to our present 4X leader,
by adding about 12 inches of 5X nylon with a Blood Knot to
the end of the leader. This makes a 10 foot leader and will fish
better than a 9 foot 5X leader. Be sure and stretch it well, so
that it will lie straight on the water.

Make your first cast upstream to the edge of the eddy. Now
the midges are really swarming and our back-eddy pocket is
boiling with big fish. You have had five good strikes and no
hooked fish; that's par for the course. If you can land one or
two big fish in an hour's fishing you're doing well. However,
you must admit, there is plenty of action.

Well, we have fished for about an hour and have three fish
between us. It's beginning to get dark and the midges have
departed as rapidly as they appeared. It is time to return to
camp.

*The fly presentation used in fishing the back eddy from posi-
tion 2, is the directly upstream cast. Part 1, Chapter III, page
22.*

# CHAPTER 9

## Opening Day

### CUT-BANK POOLS

The next trip will be on the opening day of the season. We are going to fish the cut-bank pool, Plate 4, Fig. 20. Deforestation has made this river one of great fluctuations. Sometimes it floods to such an extent that most of the native browns and rainbows are destroyed along with their spawning beds. Consequently, it is heavily stocked with hatchery innocents. The river today is moderately high, relatively clear and very cold. The water temperature is in the region of 46 to 48°. I have been warned that there have been no hatches for the past week. Two weeks ago, during a warm spell, a few Quill Gordons were seen but since then, practically no flies. This will be a wet fly situation. I am going to use my version of a Bumble Puppy . . . a streamer originally tied by Theodore Gordon to represent a minnow. I would suggest you use my all-time favorite, a #10 Bucktail Royal Coachman. We will use our sinking lines and fish this pool in the classic wet fly method, using the quartering downstream cast.

The pool is about five feet deep over by the cut-bank and along most of its length. There is a strong, relatively slow current through the pool. Because of the cold weather, the fish are apt to be against the cut-bank, deep down, in the middle portions of the pool. The bank slopes gradually to the river with plenty of room for our back casts.

We will start fishing at a point upstream outside the pic-

Fig. 20  Cutbank Pool

Plate 4

Plate 5

Plate 6

Plate 7

Plate 8

ture. We will stand at least ten feet from the water's edge.
Cast your fly to 'A,' 'B,' 'C,' in that order then walk gingerly
to fishing location 2.

Now wait a minute before you start casting to 'D,' 'E,' 'F'
and 'G.' Previously you presented your fly only at the middle
layer of the stream. These fish are probably resting on the
bottom. You have used a quartering downstream cast and allowed your fly to sweep around to a position below you. Now,
cast upstream to 'A,' 'B' and 'C' with a curved upstream cast.
This will allow your fly to sink to a deeper level. When the
line is parallel to you, strip off several feet. This will slow
your fly down and allow it to sink deeper. When the line has
reached a 45° angle below you, strip off several more feet;
your cast will be extended and your fly will slow down again
to remain deep for a bit longer. Do not strip off line too fast
as you should fish with a tight line during the downstream
phase. When fishing a wet fly, try to fish all the layers of the
water.

I have a suggestion. You fished your fly with no action. At
times, trout will want a wet fly without any action. Other
times, they want action. Most wet fly fishermen fish their flies
without action until they reach an angle of 60° below them
and then they start to pump or twitch their flies. Sometimes
it is a good idea to pump the fly from the very beginning of
the cast, varying the pumping action from small twitches to
large jerks.

*We have combined the curved upstream and the quartering
downstream casts. This can also be used with the dry fly.*

Now, it's my turn. The sun has come out and warmed up
the water; if we were to take the surface temperature I think
it would be around 50°. A few Quill Gordons are hatching.
I am going to show you an unorthodox method of fishing a

dry fly. Each year I fish this method more and more. I am
going to use my sinking line and fish a dry fly. I will prepare
my Quill Gordon with mucilin. The cast will be as usual for
dry fly fishing with an upstream curved line and no drag.
Watch carefully! The fly will float naturally until it reaches a
point about 45° below me. By this time the middle portion of
the sinking line will be down about 2 or 3 feet, depending on
the length of the cast. Drag has now developed; I will pull
the fly under and, from this point on, fish a sunk wet fly in the
middle layer of the water.

At one time I was foolish enough to think that this was a
private discovery of my own. However, Sid Gordon writes of
it in his book, "How to Fish from Top to Bottom," as does
Lee Wulff in his book, "Atlantic Salmon." It also works well
with fly fishing in trout lakes.

*Again, we have combined the curved upstream and quartering
downstream casts.*

It is your turn to try another unorthodox method. Change
your line to a floating variety. Tie a dropper roughly 4
inches in length about 4 feet from the tip of the leader,
Fig. 8, page 17. To the tip of the leader tie a wet fly or a
streamer and on the dropper tie a dry fly. Moisten the wet fly
at the tip of the leader with saliva, glycerin, soap or some other
wetting agent. Use mucilin on the dry fly attached to the
dropper. Fish this rig exactly as you would a dry fly. The tip
fly should be 2 to 3 inches under the water and the dropper fly
will ride as a conventional fly. This method is especially effective when nymphs are rising to the surface. I have had equally
good results using a large streamer as the tip fly. Many times I
have caught doubles, using this arrangement.

I'll sit on the bank and watch you.

You fished that well. There is, however, one technique you

could have added. You initially used the curved upstream cast, allowed both flies to drift past you until they started to drag, then you pulled them both under and fished them back as conventional wet flies. I find no fault with this technique. There are times, though, that you will want to use it with a nymph or a dry fly in place of the streamer at the end of the leader. In this situation you might extend the natural drift downstream as far as you can. When your flies start to drag, instead of pulling them under and fishing them as wet flies, put a small mend in your line to continue the natural drift. The downstream belly that formed in your line caused the drag. By mending it you produce an upstream belly. You may have to mend your line two or three times in the course of one drift.

We Americans do not use the line mend often enough. English fishermen are masters of it. It is essential for any technique that requires naturally drifting flies, either on top of the water or beneath. However, one word of caution! I have seen fishermen so entranced with line mending that they did it unnecessarily and too frequently, thereby putting fish down with the disturbance of their line.

Before we separate and move on to the other pools I want to review what we have done in this pool. First, you fished, quartering down and across with a sinking line; then you used a curved upstream cast and free drift to sink your line down well and then when the fly was opposite you, you stripped the line slowly from your reel and again when it was 45° below you. During this time you maintained a relatively tight line so that you could feel a fish strike.

Then I used the same technique with a dry fly and a sinking line. The first half of the cast I fished as a conventional curved upstream cast with free-floating dry fly. Then, when the fly began to drag, I pulled it under and fished it as a quartering downstream sunken fly, with a tight line.

Finally, you changed to a floating line. We discussed mending the line, using a floating line and fishing a fly with a natural drift throughout. These are the variations of combined upstream and quartering downstream casts. These variations make up a tremendous part of the essence of fly fishing.

Let us walk downstream to the next pool.


## SHALLOW RIFFLE

We have now reached a large, relatively fast, shallow riffle located between two pools. We are looking upstream at the head of this riffle. The water averages three to four feet in depth. There are medium-sized, well-covered rocks scattered throughout the water. Below us the riffle is too fast to contain many fish and we will not spend any time fishing it. For 50 feet in front of us there is slow-moving water, then it blends with the fast water. Again, there is a definite visible junction between the two currents, Plate 5, Fig. 21.

Early in the season brown and rainbow trout will inhabit a shallow riffle on sunny days because of the combination of the food and the water. The sun's rays going through the shallow water produce a warming effect much sooner than is felt in deeper water. The rocky bottom is a favorite habitat for the nymphs of the May and Stone fly all season. A hatch will develop here long before it starts in other parts of the stream.

The floating line you are fishing with is especially suitable for this stretch. Change the front fly to a Gray Nymph, the dropper fly will remain dry. Fish the dry fly and the nymph in the usual dry fly manner. Use an upstream curved cast. I will sit on the bank while you fish. The area between A and B, where the fast and slow currents join, is, as usual, a very productive region. However, the fish will be scattered throughout the riffle so be sure to fish well into the riffle, C, D, and E.

You have been fishing 15 minutes and I have counted 5

Fig. 21    Shallow Riffle

rises to your front nymph. Trout will usually not hook themselves on a naturally floating nymph. You must strike quickly
when a trout rises to your sunken nymph, in exactly the same
manner as with a dry fly. Nymph fishing is underwater dry fly
fishing. Usually you have to see the fish rise in order to hook
him. This is a fact glossed-over by most writers who describe
nymph fishing. There is another method, using a weighted
nymph deep, that we will discuss later.

Clean your fish as you catch them and you will not have
the problem of spoiled fish at the day's end. While you are
cleaning that last fish, I will tell you a few more facts about
shallow riffles.

Mid-day, late in the season, with temperatures at hot sum-

mer levels, trout will not be found in shallow riffles. They become wary and do not like the exposed position; the water temperature is too high for their liking. Then they occupy shallow riffles at dusk when it is more difficult to see them and the water is cooler.

## ROCKY RAPIDS

Slow down! You are about to pass up some of the best water on the stream! Yes, the fast rapids, depicted in Plates 6 and 7, Fig. 22, have big fish in them. They grow to a large size here. Most fishermen pass up these rapids as too fast to hold trout. The secret lies in those big rocks jutting up. Trout lie directly behind these rocks and in the slick extending 6 to 10 feet downstream. At times they also lie in the cushion of slow water directly in front. If the water is not too fast they will lie at the sides. The water here is 3 to 4 feet deep. Check your life preserver. The river can knock you off your feet and you might end in the suckholes and whirlpools in the treacherous deep pool below.

The first rock you are going to fish will be in Plate 6. Use your conventional dry fly outfit, floating line, 9-foot 2X or 3X leader. A heavier leader is necessary here because the fish usually swim out in the fast current, and break a light leader. Furthermore, the water is very turbulent and the heavier leader will not show as much as it would in slow water. Tie on a #10 irresistible. This is one of my favorite heavy water flies. It has a clipped hair body and hair wings; the same coloration as the Adams fly. It is tied so heavily that it looks like a bass bug and can be used for that purpose.

Wade out 20 feet directly below the rock. Cast into the tail end of the slick and then gradually extend your cast until your fly lands against the rock, then cast your fly close to each side of the rock.

FLOW

UNDERWATER
OBSTRUCTION

ROCK POCKET

Fig. 22    Rocky Rapids

It is easy to lose big trout in this water; therefore you must let the fish run even if it goes down into the next pool. That's why you have a hundred yards of ten-pound monofilament backing on your reel. You must play these big fish from the reel exactly as you would a steelhead or a salmon. More big fish are lost on the initial run than any other time. Usually, on reaching that big pool below, they will make a jump. When they do, lower the tip of your rod. This will help to prevent the hook from being torn out of the fish's mouth.

Next, wade to a point just opposite the rock about 30 feet out from it. Tie on a weighted may fly nymph and cast it directly behind the rock. Allow it to drift directly through the swift water without drag.

No luck? Now, wade slowly and carefully to a point directly above the rock. Rest that water for at least ten minutes. Now, tie on a #10 bucktail stone fly. First, fish it as a downstream dry fly along both sides of the rock and then into the slick. When you bring it back, try easing it on top of the water and pull it through the slick with little twitches. At times, this will drive trout crazy and at other times it will put them down. A bouncing spider fly is particularly deadly with this technique. Both techniques work well at times. The spider fly will work better in clear, calm water.

Still no luck? Put a split shot at the head of your fly. Remember there is not much difference in appearance between a stonefly nymph and a stonefly. Sunk, it looks like the nymph, especially in fast water. Now, fish it through the slick as you would a streamer.

A weighted fly is a lethal weapon; when you fish a weighted fly wear a hat and a pair of polaroid glasses. Had Ambassador Lewis Douglas worn a pair, while fishing on a Scottish salmon river, he probably would not have lost an eye when it was struck by a weighted fly.

### ROCKY REACH

Upstream from here is a beautiful rocky reach, Plate 8, Fig. 23. What is a rocky reach? The word 'reach' is an English term loosely applied to a fishable stretch of water lying between two well-defined pools. The water may be fast, slow, full of rocks, etc. It conjures up the picture of an English gentleman, complete with tweed knickers and cap, fishing Lord Havershaw's Reach on the Itchin with his gilly waiting patiently just behind him. I have always wanted a gilly but I don't know what I'd do with him . . . have him carry the beer? Or make excuses for my fishing?

This stretch could best be defined as a shallow rocky reach.

Fig. 23   Rocky Reach

On a bright day such as this the fish would be lying in the shadows of the rocks and close in at their sides. The water is relatively slow and clear. I would suggest, when you do fish this, that you use a long line (a minimum of 30 feet and, even better, 50 feet) and a light 5X leader. Remember, the longer the line that you can use practically, the more chance you have of catching big, wary fish. Err on the side of too long a cast. If you can see a fish he usually can see you!

Fish this in exactly the same manner that you did the Rocky Rapids . . . except for a long line.

# CHAPTER 10

## Some Things Easily Missed

### HIDDEN POOL

The next section of the stream we shall fish consists of a pool that can be easily missed unless the fisherman is alert to its possibilities. Above and below this pool are two large, typical, deep curved pools. Both are obvious and are fished very heavily. In between these two pools is a straight stretch of shallow, fast rapids averaging one to two feet in depth and about 80 feet in width. As we walk down this stretch and reach a point about midway between the two large pools, we will notice an area where the water becomes darker in appearance and the rate of flow slightly lower, Plate 9. A careful scrutiny reveals a shallow pool, about 75 feet long. From the spot on which we are standing the bottom slopes downward until it reaches a maximum depth of about 5 feet at approximately 2 feet from the opposite shore. The bank on the opposite shore is very steep but is not undercut. To fish this stretch from the other shore is difficult and almost impossible. It is not practical to wade upstream. To stand on the bank and cast any distance upstream is out of the question because of the shrubbery on the edge of the bank. Floting a long line downstream with many 'S' curves is possible but very difficult. Most of the trout in this stream will know you are there by the vibration you set up as you attempt to fish downstream. The most deadly manner in which to fish this area is from the side we are standing on.

About ten feet behind us are pine trees so we must wade

out about 20 feet to have enough room for a back cast. It is
true that a good roll caster might stand on the edge of the
bank and cast across but, in this situation, the longer the line
the quicker it will develop drag. I want you to fish this first
with a dry fly. Start fishing and gradually work your fly across
to the opposite bank; then move upstream and repeat.

No fish! And no evident fly hatch! We are going to have to
change our tactics. However, before we do this, I want to re-
emphasize what a deadly technique is fishing from one bank
to the other. This is what makes boat fishing so effective. The
ability to float slowly downstream and cast to either shore will
often produce fish when bank fishermen have nothing for their
pains but empty creels.

Our present situation requires a deeply sunk nymph. Come
sit on the bank with me and we will discuss nymph and nymph
fly fishing.

All the techniques we have discussed in this book on fly
presentation apply to nymph fishing. You can even grease one
of these flies and fish it as a dry fly. Don't forget that a May
Fly Nymph does float on the surface while the Dun is breaking
out of its shell.

Most nymph flies and nymphs are tied on heavy hooks.
These are nothing but standard hooks made of thicker wire.
However, they will sink somewhat faster than conventional
hooks. Commonly, the nymph is fished under water, without
drag, in exactly the same manner as the dry fly. It should be
fished in varying water depths. The true nymph experts fish
with a 9 or 12 foot sinking leader and a floating line.

There is one major problem in nymph fishing. Getting the
nymph down! This form of fishing is most effective on slow-
moving brown trout streams. I am convinced that the brown
trout is a better taker of nymphs than his cousin the rainbow.
Many Eastern brown trout experts, fishing in private club

waters, will locate a large brown trout in such water and then, after much thought, will organize a deliberate campaign, stalk the fish and catch him with a nymph.

Enough talk! This is a rainbow stream. The current in the hidden pool is not too swift to fish a nymph in the conventional manner.

You sit on the bank and I will demonstrate.

I will wade out as you did before. I have cast quartering upstream, the nymph and leader are now sinking and I judge that it is about three feet under the water. Now it is opposite me and I will gradually lift it out of the water. Wham! I have hooked one, old Leisenring's technique worked. The fish was a beauty but he is off now. He certainly stirred up this pool. I will sit down and rest it for a spell.

The lift I used was originated by the late Jim Leisenring who perfected nymph flies. At any time in the drift of the nymph one simply raises the fly rod upward; this makes the nymph rise deliberately to the surface. This maneuver imitates natural nymphs rising to the surface to hatch. It is very difficult to perform this maneuver in fast water.

How do you get a nymph down in fast water? Use a nymph tied with a lead wire body. They are miserable things to cast and lose their life-like qualities when floating in the water.

The late Jim Quick in his book on nymph fishing described two methods of fishing a deeply-sunk fly. First, a four-inch dropper is tied about two-and-a-half to three feet above the nymph. To this is attached several split shots; or, a simpler method is to place two or three split shots about the same distance up the leader. Now the fun begins!! The experts speak knowingly of striking when there is a pause in the drift of the leader, or maintaining sufficient tension on the line to feel the strike.

Fishing a weighed nymph, to me, is akin to lure or bait

fishing. I do it at times because I like to catch trout but I do not get the sense of achievement from this method that I get when I fish a nymph fly with no weight.

What has held back nymph fishing from being as popular as other methods of fly fishing? It is a difficult technique to master.

When the fly is much below a foot in depth, it is difficult to see or feel the trout strike. The freely-drifting nymph is the most effective but in fast water it is a problem sinking it to any depth. If the nymph is weighted enough to get it to the proper depth, it then loses its ability to float freely and naturally. Trout are more finicky about color, size and shape in ideal nymph water than they are about dry and wet flies that are fished in the conventional manner.

With all the difficulties found in nymph and nymph fly fishing I have never met a truly great fisherman who did not agree that the nymph fly and nymph, fished with a natural free drift, is the deadliest method for catching trout. When sufficient fishermen learn to use the nymph properly, our streams could really become fished-out. There is one satisfaction: by the time a fisherman gains these skills, he has long ago become a fish returner.

Shall we walk down to the next stretch?

## UNDERCUT BANKS

This section of stream consists of a long stretch of water in a large river. On the left, 100 yards upriver there is an island. Behind us the river continues on a straight down-stream course, for approximately 20 yards, where it gradually shallows to about six inches.

The factor that makes this section a terrific fish producer is the undercut bank, see Plate 10, Fig. 24. The undercut varies in depth one to two feet. The river flow is relatively fast and

the bottom is rocky. Where we are standing the depth of the water is about four feet.

How are we going to fish this?

The best method is either to wade out from the opposite bank, as we did in the last pool, or fish it from a boat about 50 feet from the shore. However, the river is about six feet deep in this region and, fortunately for the river, no boat fishing is allowed. Standing on the bank and fishing upstream will work but it necessitates a cast over the left shoulder. Silhouetted against the sky you are visible to the trout for a radius of 20 to 30 feet. This visibility cuts down on the amount of fishable water. One satisfactory method of fishing this is by wading.

First, we will try a dry fly. Start fishing directly upstream. From this location place your fly as close to the bank as possible and then work it out from the edge gradually. Keep your eyes open as the fish will many times swim out from the bank and feed on natural flies toward the middle.

The dry fly does not work? Then try fishing a nymph fly upstream.

You have now worked your way upstream about 100 yards and have been fortunate enough to catch and release several nice fish. What a beautiful day and what a nice stretch of stream.

Now, go fish another stretch of water for about a half an hour and allow this to rest; we will then come back to this stretch and fish downstream with a sunken streamer fly.

The half hour has passed and we are ready to go at it again. The average fisherman who attempts to wade this will simply wade downstream and the result will be no fish. The proper method is as follows:

When you approach the bank you should be at least 25 yards away from it then walk directly in as gently as possible. Step quietly into the water, don't fish . . . just stand absolutely still for 5 minutes or more, then false cast about 15 feet of line.

CROSS SECTION

Fig. 24   Undercut Bank

Plate 9

Plate 10

Work out the remainder of the needed line. At first, work about 20 feet of line out and bring it back with little jerks. Next, cast quartering from the bank until you have worked the middle section of the stream. Now, let out more line and repeat the process. After you have fished over about 50 feet of the stream you will be ready to go downstream. Do not wade! Climb out on the bank, walk back 50 feet, then walk downstream about ⅔ the distance that your line and fly previously covered then walk directly in and repeat the process of waiting and then fishing. In this manner the fish will not hear and feel the vibrations of your walking.

You can also use this same S curve method with a long line and fish a dry fly without drag downstream.

# CHAPTER 11

## *Middle of July*

### MID-DAY FISHING

The time is the middle of July, and we are camped along a lovely river. Because we arrived at camp in the small hours of the morning, we both agreed to sleep late. By the time we have finished breakfast, done our camp chores, it is about 10:30 in the morning. Consequently, we will do most of our fishing in the mid-day period.

I prefer mid-day fishing because most of the other fishermen have retired from the river.

There is no accounting for fly hatches or fish feeding periods. During the summer months there is usually a hatch sometime during the day; most often between 10:00 a.m. and 2.00 p.m.

There is a secret to mid-day fishing during the summer. It can be summed up in one word, 'SHADE.' Trout seek the shade for two reasons. They are less visible to their enemies and they frequently find food under the shade of trees. The awaited mid-day hatch may not come off, however, caddis, stone flies and may flies that have been hatched at a previous time collect under the leaves and branches of shade trees during the warm, sunny periods of the day. At times, they become active and frequently fall or fly down to the water. The trout, being aware of this, will wait under the shade trees for this bounty of food. This phenomenon may occur during the mid-day on dull, overcast days.

Let's go up to Hinton's Flat and look at the river. Now

look at Plates 11 and 12, Fig. 25. This is mid-day water. Notice the patches of shade under the trees and grass clumps. There goes an olive Dun off the water! There goes another! There . . . a good fish just rose! What are we waiting for?

Use a short line and a side-arm cast to put your fly up under those trees. You are going to have to wade upstream and crouch under the trees to do it.

If the hatch under those trees peters out don't spend a great deal of time fishing that water . . . keep moving! During the mid-day period a stretch of water may be completely dead while around the bend great activity may be taking place.

In contrast, at dusk, pick a likely stretch of water and stay with it. The best period of dusk-fishing usually lasts only half an hour and you may miss it going from place to place.

Remember . . . mid-day fishing . . . keep moving!

## DAPPING

On your way back upstream, stop at that pocket I showed you earlier in the day, Plate 12, Fig. 25. That is a marvelous spot for dapping. What do I mean by dapping? That's the same as piddle-fishing! You kind of piddle your fly in the water. Clear, isn't it?

Dapping is an old English term that goes back to the roots of fly fishing. I believe Isaac Walton and Joseph Cotton spoke of dapping.

You sneak up to about 6 or 8 feet from the bank, extend your rod out over the bank with just enough line so that your fly will land on the water, float a foot or so and then quietly lift it off the water and repeat the process.

In the spot shown on Plate 12, Fig. 25, kneel or even lie on your belly about four or five feet back from the bank parallel to the bush with the flowers. Extend your rod tip out and drop your fly right next to those yellow flowers, then gradually

Fig. 25   Mid-day Water

extend your fly until it floats in the white water. When you have fished that out, walk downstream about 30 feet, slide into the water and cast your fly up against the lower side of the clump of grass just above the bush with the flowers. I saw a large trout rise there last night. I am sure he is still there.

Another spot that is ideal for dapping is shown in Plate 11, Fig. 25. Instead of wading up under those trees and casting to that big rock, tiptoe out on the bank to a point 6 feet from the bank and dapp your fly right behind it. This is the only way that you can fish some brushy spots.

## MOSS BANK HOLE

We have finished dapping and darkness is upon us and we are walking back to camp.

You asked me earlier in the day about chalk streams and whether we have them in this country. Chalk streams are found in England. They are typically slow, meandering streams that flow through and out of chalk deposits. The water is a deep blue, and at times they are literally choked with vegetation. They support a tremendous amount of insect life. The English differentiate between chalk and limestone streams. The actual difference between these streams is more geologic. The water is similar in both streams. What makes these streams such tremendous fish producers is the hardness or actual lime content of the water. The hardness of the water determines the amount of insect life that can thrive in a stream and, thus, the number of fish it will support. Sid Gordon, in his book "How to Fish from Top to Bottom," explains this in great detail and gives simple methods of chemical analysis for the lime content of water.

For years American fishing writers denied the existence of chalk or limestone streams in this country. They were wrong. There are not any true chalk streams but typical limestone

streams do exist in parts of the middle west and Pennsylvania. The LeTorte in Pennsylvania is a limestone stream and looks like a typical chalk stream. I am told that if one were to blindfold the late Skues, father of the modern nymph, and drop him on the LeTorte, he would think he was still fishing one of his own beloved English chalk streams. Charles Fox's book, "This Wonderful World of Trout" describes this stream in full detail.

I have never knowingly fished a true limestone stream. Silver Creek, a hard-water stream in Idaho, comes close to fitting this description. The river we will fish tomorrow is classified as semi-hard water. In a few spots it presents some of the typical aspects of very-hard water.

Morning is upon us and we have driven over to the moss bank hole. The word 'moss' is bandied about loosely by fishermen. The so-called 'moss bed' you see in Plate 13, Fig. 26, is not moss at all but made up of true aquatic plants that are commonly called water weeds. These particular weeds provide an excellent nursery for aquatic insects, snails, plankton, shrimp, etc.

When I took this picture the river was high enough to completely cover the moss or weed bed. Look carefully at the Plate and you will notice an irregular coloration extending out from the shore into the river. This is the 'moss' or weed bed. Later in the season the tips of the weeds will be visible. Trout like to lie right up against the weeds.

When you fish this hole cast upstream and place your fly at the edge of the moss bank. The water is too deep to wade at the outer edge of the moss bed, so you must wade up through the moss. You must wade carefully. The velocity of the water is slow in amongst the weeds and trout will be able to hear you for a long distance both up and down stream. It can be waded downstream by the method described in the Undercut Bank section of this book.

Fig. 26  Moss Bed Pool

Aquatic plants are not always desirable in a stream. It is possible to introduce the wrong plants into a stream and ruin it by actually choking up the stream. Even in some of the best chalk and limestone streams in England, the proper plants become too thick and they must be thinned-out at certain times of the year in order to maintain good fishing.

Every four or five years the moss beds in Silver Creek, Idaho, wash out and with them go the fish . . . much to the consternation of the fishermen. I wonder if this is not Nature's way of keeping this stream in a healthy state?

I can see you are impatient to start fishing this stretch. Good luck and wade slowly and carefully. Don't get discouraged if most of the fish run into the weeds and break you off.

## MUDDY WATER

This morning fishing conditions are not very auspicious. A sudden rain last night sent the stream up about 6 inches. The water is muddy, about the color of coffee. This situation is not as bad as it first appears. If you will look carefully at the bank you will notice that the water has fallen about an inch.

This is a beautiful, sunny, middle-of-June day and the time of the largest may fly hatches for these streams. The sun is just beginning to warm the water and already a few Red Uprights can be seen. In the past I have had fine fishing in just this situation . . . falling water, plus a large fly hatch, usually produces fine dry fly fishing, no matter the color of the water. If a white china plate is visible 2 feet beneath the surface, good fly fishing is possible. The murkier the water, the more thoroughly one must fish any given stretch. Trout in crystal clear water can see a fly within a radius of 20 to 30 feet; in very muddy water they must be within 6 inches of it and close to the surface. Hence, we must lengthen our casts 6 to 12 inches with each successive cast to fully cover the water.

Plate 11

Plate 12

Plate 13

Plate 14

Paradoxically, this is also true in very cold (40-50°), clear water when trout are at the bottom. In this type of water they can see the fly but they are so sluggish that they will not bother to swim more than a few inches. This is particularly true of Winter Steelhead.

Let us suppose there are no obvious flies visible on the water, no trout rising and the water is coffee-colored. What then? Bait is a logical choice, but I simply have no fun catching trout on bait. This is a situation for a large streamer fly; a #6 or even, at times, a #4. I use my old friend, the Bucktail Royal Coachman or a large streamer fly with a maribou wing. If this does not work, then a fluorescent fly will often turn the trick. I don't consider this a true fly . . . but a lure. It may be necessary to place a split shot ahead of the fly or use a weighted fly. A quartering downstream cast is used. Fish the usual areas where one would expect to find trout but also fish the quiet regions where you would not usually bother. Mr. Hewitt, in his classic book "Telling on Trout," writes of catching trout in the grass of the meadows that border the Neversink River at flood stages. They also seem to like the tail-end of pools at this time.

Well, a good two hours have passed. The water is still falling. Let's get on with our fishing.

## ISLANDS

Today is the end of our fishing together. I have saved one of my favorite spots for our last trip. This will be a short trip and we will spend only a few hours fishing the island, Plate 14, Fig. 27. The largest fish I have caught have been around islands. We will wade out to this island; check your life preserver!

Where do you want to start fishing? The water on the left looking upstream is excellent, especially behind the rocks near

the large tree. The shadow from that large tree will provide ample shade. This picture was taken about 4:00 o'clock in the afternoon on a mid-summer day. Shadows are present on the water just at the edge of the rocks. On the right side of the

Fig. 27   Island

island is a typical riffle with the characteristic meeting of fast and slow water. Your comments on how to fish this are correct, however, you have missed the best location for big fish . . . the tail-end of the island. An island is nothing but a big rock. More trout hold behind a rock than do at the sides or at the front. Examine Figure 27 . . . carefully! Where the two currents come together downstream, is the hotspot for big trout. Unfortunately, it is not shown in the picture and you must

rely on the drawing. The biggest trout I have ever caught have been in this location.

First, cast a dry fly downstream with big 'S' curves in the line about three feet above the hotspot, and allow your fly to drift down until drag develops. I particularly like to fish this spot with a dry fly and a sinking line. By the time the fly starts to drag, the line has sunk down quite a good distance. Then, bring it back with little jerks as a sunk wet fly. When the fly is in the region of the hotspot allow it to hang for a few minutes. Some anglers keep their fly in this location for as long as five or ten minutes before finally bringing it in.

You fish this area and I will commence fishing on the left side of the island and work my way upstream. You should spend at least one-half-hour working the tail of the island. When you have finished this, then fish that riffle to the right.

# Fishing Addages

## GOOD FISHING

1. Rising barometer.
2. Falling water.
3. Dark of the moon.

## POOR FISHING

1. East wind.
2. Falling barometer.
3. Rising water.
4. First bright day after several dark or rainy days (or vice versa).
5. Full moon.
6. Thunder.

As I bring this book to a close, I feel as if I have lost a real fishing partner. In the future, if you have a fishing problem that I might be able to help you with, please drop me a note. *Be sure you enclose a stamped, self-addressed envelope.*

Do not ask me where to go fishing. I cannot abide people that exploit particular fishing streams by writing about them. The various state fish and game commissions can give you that information.

GOOD LUCK!!
Lenox Dick
833 - S.W. 11th Ave.
Portland, Oregon 97205

# Index